THE FOUR INTELLIGENCES OF THE BUSINESS MIND

HOW TO REWIRE YOUR BRAIN AND YOUR BUSINESS FOR SUCCESS

Valeh Nazemoff

Ca technologies

CA Press

Apress®

The Four Intelligences of the Business Mind: How to Rewire Your Brain and Your Business for Success

Managing Director: Welmoed Spahr
Acquisitions Editor: Robert Hutchinson
Technical Reviewer: Erik Hille
Editorial Board: Steve Anglin, Mark Beckner, Ewan Buckingham, Gary Cornell,
    Louise Corrigan, James DeWolf, Jonathan Gennick, Robert Hutchinson,
    Michelle Lowman, James Markham, Matthew Moodie, Jeff Olson, Jeffrey Pepper,
    Douglas Pundick, Ben Renow-Clarke, Dominic Shakeshaft, Gwenan Spearing,
    Matt Wade, Steve Weiss
Coordinating Editor: Rita Fernando
Copy Editor: Ann Dickson, Jennifer Sharpe
Compositor: SPi Global
Indexer: SPi Global
Cover Designer: Anna Ishchenko

Distributed to the book trade worldwide by Springer Science+Business Media, LLC., 233 Spring Street, 6th Floor, New York, NY 10013. Phone 1-800-SPRINGER, fax (201) 348-4505, e-mail orders-ny@springer-sbm.com, or visit www.springeronline.com.

For information on translations, please e-mail rights@apress.com, or visit www.apress.com.

Apress and friends of ED books may be purchased in bulk for academic, corporate, or promotional use. eBook versions and licenses are also available for most titles. For more information, reference our Special Bulk Sales–eBook Licensing web page at www.apress.com/bulk-sales.

I dedicate this book to you, the reader, on your journey forward to success. Success is the ripple effect that you cause in society through your actions. The most successful actions are rooted in positive intention, proactive initiation, inspiring innovation, and improvement of self and others.
Let's impact the world together!

Contents

Foreword

In the world of neuroscience, to which I've devoted the last ten years of my life, big ideas can change the structure and functioning of your brain in extraordinarily positive ways. And when you communicate your big ideas—and the values they embrace—to other people, you change their brain as well. Perhaps most importantly, when you bring your deepest values and new ideas into your work and business, you can begin to transform the world. Values like love, compassion, integrity, and trust can build stronger relationships among lovers, friends, and colleagues.

But you must do so consciously, and you must do so on a daily basis. That is why, each year, I ask my Executive MBA students who are enrolled in my NeuroLeadership class the following question: "What is your deepest innermost value?" My students ask themselves this question every morning for ten days. The result: 90% report less stress at work, more productivity, and greater joy.

Big ideas can literally add years of happiness to your life, easing anxiety and bringing inner peace. Valeh Nazemoff's *The Four Intelligences of the Business Mind* is a big idea, and a great one. Most businesses aim for success by doing better at what they already do. This is an admirable goal, but it's not a game changer. Game-changing ideas come from noticing and meeting the unmet needs of your customers, your partners, and your colleagues within your own organization. In this book, Ms. Nazemoff shows you the path to finding those unmet needs and creating game-changing products and services to solve them.

One of the things I love about this book is how the author integrates her business expertise with the latest evidence from the world of neuroscience. Why? Because we now know enough about the brain to improve the way we conduct business in the world. If you ignore the neuroscientific principles presented in this book, you limit the success of your work.

One of the most important ideas that Valeh emphasizes is the concept of using what she calls your "Business Mind." You use your Business Mind by integrating all of the cognitive skills that are scattered throughout many regions of your brain: your logic centers, your data centers, your emotional centers, your creative centers, and—most important—your intuitive centers located in the newest evolutionary parts of the brain.

Most people, and thus most organizations, tend to use only one or two of these "business brain" skills. They may emphasize facts but lack inspiration, or they use their intuition or imagination—it's often hard to tell which is which—and come up with ideas that aren't practical. As a neuroscience researcher, I know that every hypothesis—which often comes from intuition, not logic—needs data, and I'm glad Valeh is bringing this idea to the world of business.

The bigger problem, in both science and business, is knowing what problems to solve. This is where the Four Intelligences of the Business Mind come in. As she helps you understand the concepts of Financial, Customer, Data, and Mastermind Intelligence, Valeh leads you through a group of actions that you need to take in order to implement them. If you follow her suggestions, you will find out what items in your business need to transform, and how to transform them.

If you want to achieve the highest level of transformation, however, you can't just stay inside the bubble of your own business and its customers; you have to look at the world at large. Valeh gives you the tools you need to discover patterns in the outside world. These patterns will lead you to opportunities for your business that you couldn't find otherwise. You can often fulfill unmet needs of customers on a much larger scale when you keep your eye on the world at large.

One of my favorite things about this book is the idea of bringing the philosophy behind a mastermind session to your organization on a full-time basis. Two of the cornerstones of a mastermind session are brainstorming and acceptance. First, you want to come up with as many ideas as possible. As a group, you all pledge to listen to all ideas without judgment. If every company were to take this creative approach, I suspect many more of the world's problems could be solved.

Finally, Valeh suggests a level of inclusiveness that is rarely practiced in the business world. She advises that you include someone from any department that is affected by any issue you are looking to solve, even if that issue is only a small part of their work. The goal is to filter new plans through as many lenses as possible to come up with optimal programs and also to avoid unforeseen consequences.

That sounds like good science to me.

I highly recommend that you look at your organization through the lens of *The Four Intelligences of the Business Mind*. If you do so, your business will improve in unexpected ways.

—Mark Waldman
Executive MBA Faculty
Loyola Marymount University

About the Author

 **Valeh Nazemoff** is Senior Vice President and Co-Owner of Acolyst, a technology services and business consultancy company. She is recognized as a strategic advisor, management consultant, team builder, speaker, author, and teacher. Nazemoff has guided project teams for many government clients, including the U.S. Postal Service, Social Security Administration, and Pension Benefit Guaranty Corporation. She has consulted for clients of CA Technologies, been engaged by Lockheed Martin and CACI International, and coached and conducted workshops which included attendees from Harvard University, IBM, Walmart, and Erie Insurance. She has taught and mentored students from George Mason University, the University of Mary Washington, the University of Phoenix, and Marymount University on various business topics and skills. Nazemoff has a BS in psychology and MBAs in e-business and global management from the University of Phoenix. She is based in the Washington, D.C., metro area. The author invites comments and inquiries at valeh.nazemoff@acolyst.com.

About the Technical Reviewer

Erik Hille is Senior Principal Product Marketing Manager, CA Technologies. An authority in the areas of ITIL's Service Level Management, Service Portfolio Management and Service Catalog Management processes, he previously served as the marketing director of Oblicore, product marketing director at ATG, and director of Internet research at Roper Starch/ASW. Hille took his BA in psychology and MBA in marketing from the University of Missouri.

Acknowledgments

Every day, I am filled with gratitude for the opportunities that I've been given time and time again. I am most grateful to my mother, for her endless support and belief in me. Thank you for your unconditional love. You are my inspiration and my greatest mentor. I am humbled to have learned so much from you in business and in life.

This book could not have been brought to the world without the incredibly supportive and forward thinking CA Press team at CA Technologies. Thank you to Adam Famularo, Karen Sleeth, Erik Hille, Connie Smallwood, Derek Stevens, the CA Legal team, and the many reviewers who devoted time from their very busy schedules to make this book a reality. A special thanks also goes to the many other all-stars at CA Technologies, such as Wendy Petty, Andi Mann, George Watt, Donna Burbank, Kathy Meara, Marjorie Martinez, Rick Alaras, Chris Kreiling, Robert DeSilva, Sean Aryai, Ron Collier, Diana Parks, Eric Feldman, Denise Dubie, Penni Geller, Sabra Jan Willner, and Andrew Spoeth.

I would like to also offer heartfelt gratitude to the amazing group at Apress who believed that this book would make a difference in society. Special thanks to the superbly amazing Robert Hutchinson for helping *The Four Intelligences* find its voice. Rita Fernando, you are a joy to work with, and I thank you for keeping me on schedule and within guidelines. And I can't forget to mention the rest of the team who worked tirelessly behind the scenes: Jeff Olson, Jennifer Sharpe, Ann Dickson, Dhaneesh Kumar, and many others.

I am grateful and thankful to Tracy Grigoriades for the countless hours and enthusiasm in supporting me to bring this message to the world.

Many experts contributed significantly to this book, providing invaluable life lessons, sharing ideas and support, and helping me refine my vision: Steve Harrison, Mahesh Grossman, Martha Bullen, Brian Edmondson, Raia King, Danette Kubanda, Geoffrey Berwind, Debra Englander, John Assaraf, and Jack Canfield.

Thanks to the insight and wisdom of Mark Waldman and Jacqueline Hadden, for enlightening me and being there for me from the very beginning.

Thank you to the interviewees, friends, and colleagues who enthusiastically made themselves available throughout this process: Curtis Coy, Gary Quinn, Janet Wood, Paul Zak, and Cary Bayer.

To my early readers, Alan Komet, Chuck Corjay, Shaun Khalfan, James Brady, and Joe Distefano—your positive and excited reactions to my early chapters meant so much to me.

I have been blessed to have so many inspirational mentors, influencers, sponsors, and champions come into my life—George Kafkarkou, Jim Tedesco, Bob Otto, Beth Berger, Lorena Costanza, Vaughn Harman, Tracy Balent, Larry Walsh, Heather Clancy, Nancy Hammervik, Teresa Varela-Lauper, Jennifer Follett, Robert Faletra, Robert DeMarzo, Steve Burke, Herb Siegel, Ken Manning, Dave Weetman, Robert Fake, George Janis, Greg Fortunato, Mike Namvar, my teachers, and other authors.

Thank you to my students and those that I have mentored and coached over the years. Thank you for giving me the opportunity to guide and be of service. Thank you also to my friends near and in Bayside, Fenwick Island, Delaware, where I spent most of my time writing this book.

The inspiration for *The Four Intelligences of the Business Mind* would not have happened if not for my clients, with whom I travel on this wonderful journey.

I am also so grateful to our veterans. Because of you, I have the freedom, as a woman, to express, write, and share my thoughts and opinions. Many women are not so fortunate in other parts of the world, but I am hopeful one day this will change.

Thanks to my brother, Kaveh Nazemoff, for your creative energy. Thanks to my family and friends who graciously and patiently waited as I worked on this book, knowing how important it was for me to share this message. Through your understanding of my crazy schedule and spotty attendance at events, you showed your true love to me. I love you all.

Special thanks to my grandmother. You are my heart and my soul. Thank you for being the female entrepreneur that many aspire to be. You have given to so many and changed so many lives. I can only dream to live up to your reputation of giving endlessly with no expectation in return.

Thanks to the angels who helped guide me to creativity and inspiration when I had writer's block—which happened often.

And thank you, Universe, for bringing it all together in sometimes unexplainable ways.

Your Brain, Mind, and Business Transformation

It is not enough to have a good mind. The main thing is to use it well.

—René Descartes, *Le Discours de la Méthode*

Information overload is the new normal. We have too much to think about and too little time to manage the rush of information coming at us from multiple sources. The nonstop tsunami of structured and unstructured data that slams into our lives throughout our waking hours—and, for some of us, throughout our sleeping hours—can adversely affect our clarity of thought and, thus, our decision-making abilities. As such, it has become a monumental challenge for executives and decision-makers to keep themselves and their teams focused on doing the right things and on making the best business decisions.

It's also extremely difficult to change or transform your business when you don't know what to focus on first, where to start, and how best to view things. Organizational transformation impacts people, processes, technology, and information. It comes in different styles, shapes, and forms, whether in the guise of a merger or acquisition, a new initiative or program, a consolidation of internal departments, or a reduction of unnecessary administrative costs. Transformation may be centered on a department, a division, an entire enterprise, or across multiple companies.

But before you can begin the process of transforming your business, you and your employees must develop the right mindset.

The Brain and Transformational Intelligence

What is that mindset?

In order to describe it, we need to discuss how the brain works. Certain parts of the brain are analytic, others are intuitive, other parts are social, and some are just plain anxious. The key is to realize where your own brain fits into the scheme. The rule that every individual is defined as a composite of strengths in some areas and weaknesses in others extends to all the multifarious facets of the human brain, mind, and consciousness.

How do you base your decisions? Do you consider yourself more intuitive or analytical? If you're an intuitive decision maker, you base your decisions on "feelings" that you get. Your ideas come from bursts of creativity. If you're an analytical decision maker, you base your decisions on historical data. You crunch the numbers that your business generates and extract patterns from them. Then you use those patterns to change course as needed.

The problem is that neither of these modalities, when used separately, will transform your business. Ideas that come from a burst of creativity, like the kind that employees spontaneously throw out in the middle of a meeting, often are not supported by data. Ideas based on data often involve doing either more, or less, of something you're already doing, rather than being based on something new.

The best way to accomplish transformation in your organization is to use an approach that combines both intuitive and analytical thinking. This creates what I call "Transformational Intelligence."

What makes Transformational Intelligence different from ordinary intelligence is that you use the whole brain, as opposed to using your brain only in the way that comes naturally to you. Organizations are most successful when a company culture is created where everyone works this way, not just you. Transformational Intelligence uses neuroscience, psychology, organizational behavior, and analytics to drive and transform business performance, while improving collaboration and communication. It helps decision makers and executives drive value by providing a framework to define strategic initiatives, improve financial goals, exceed customer satisfaction, streamline business processes and tools, and motivate employees to become innovative and creative.

The Four Essential Transformational Intelligences for Business

There are four core areas where Transformational Intelligence has the biggest effect. Each of these areas requires its own particular Transformational Intelligence:

- **Financial Intelligence**: The ability to collect and use financial data to generate insights that inform intelligent decision making regarding items like cash flow, profitability, and growth, as well as quality and productivity.

- **Customer Intelligence**: The understanding of who your customers are and how to attract, find, reach, and connect with them, through the lenses of sales and marketing, customer support and services, and partner and supplier relationships.

- **Data Intelligence**: The creation of standardized internal processes, procedures, systems, and activities across an organization made transparent and universally comprehended through collaboration and the communication of timely visual data. This cohesive approach enables transformative, value-creating decisions.

- **Mastermind Intelligence**: The brainstorming of ideas and solutions in a nonjudgmental, well-respected environment. It is about empowering employees to be innovative, engaging partners and customers, and finding ways to support those partners and customers you've connected with.

These intelligences are all interlinked. Financial Intelligence requires Customer Intelligence, otherwise there won't be any money coming in. Customer Intelligence requires the transformative decisions enabled by Data Intelligence in order to create the value that brings in customers. Data Intelligence needs Mastermind Intelligence in order to act on the information that is discovered by collaboration throughout the organization. Mastermind Intelligence loops back to Financial Intelligence, to assess the financial requirements of the actions created by Mastermind Intelligence, since everything an organization implements requires either money or a reallocation of manpower and resources.

These Four Transformational Intelligences were shaped by the work I've done with organizations over the past 15 years, as well as lessons I've learned from my colleagues and mentors. Time and again, the solutions I helped put into place boiled down to these four aspects of intelligence. Here are a few highlights:

- The management of a $65-billion government organization was consistently given too much data and not enough usable information. This happened because no one had figured out which data was relevant. Also, when faced with legislative mandates, the organization didn't know what the impact would be and where to apply changes. Using the Four Transformational Intelligences, this agency was able to reduce cost, cater to their internal customers (marketing, human resources, and finance), gain visual insight, and communicate effectively with their employees. They also have a process for continuous improvement.

- Because of a government mandate, an insurance risk management organization needed to merge and consolidate processes across multiple departments to respond to their customers' needs. These changes affected many internal employees, contractors, and consultants. They were experiencing friction, misdirection, and costly rework before I became actively involved. After working through the Four Transformational Intelligences, there was clarity, structure, organization, and collaboration across the board.

- The CEO of an international software company needed to expand business into a new industry. By using the Four Transformational Intelligences, the company successfully broke into the new niche.

I have applied the Four Transformational Intelligences to a wide variety of businesses with a plethora of different needs. Those organizations had and are continuing to have tremendous breakthroughs. I've had enough success with this system to know that it can work for you too. That's why I'm bringing it to you in this book.

Using the Four Transformational Intelligences, you will learn how to declutter, simplify, collaborate, communicate, and strategize better. You will change the way you look at your processes, patterns, behaviors, and thinking habits so that you make better business decisions, where the transformation process becomes less painful and more productive.

Brain and Mind

The following chapters will delve into each of these Four Transformational Intelligences and how to implement them in your organization. First, however, it's important that you understand how the human brain and mind work; how we process information, what ignites and triggers our behaviors, and how we make decisions. The more you know and understand how you and the people within your organization function at the most basic level, the greater insight you'll have as you seek to transform your business.

To many, including scientists and psychologists, the terms *brain* and *mind* are interchangeable because you can't have one without the other. In fact, there is no single agreed-upon definition of "the mind." In the context of this book, however, I distinguish between the two. The brain is the physical organ, part of the central nervous system, situated within the skull. It enables you to have a mind. The mind refers to the part of you that is capable of thinking, sensing, and performing higher functions such as reason, memory, decision-making, and emotion.

The Executive Functions of the Brain

The sophisticated, complex, and enchanting organ known as the brain weighs in at two to three pounds. It gives us boundless potential and grand powers because it is what gives us the ability to use our mind.

The two hemispheres of mammalian brains are encased in a thin rind of neural tissue called the *cerebral cortex*. In human beings, most of the cerebral cortex is a six-layered structure called the *neocortex*, which is the most highly developed of cerebral tissues and the most recently evolved, hence the prefix "neo." The neocortex is divided into four regions called lobes that are mapped by the four largest sutured bones of the cranial vault. Accordingly, the *frontal, parietal, temporal,* and *occipital lobes* (Figure 1-1) are the regions of your neocortex that lie under your frontal, parietal, temporal, and occipital skull bones.

The neocortex enables higher functions of conscious thought, sensory insight, motor commands, spatial reasoning, and language. It is the part of the brain that enables us to predict who we'll be bumping into at the water cooler, what we'll be hearing at today's meeting, and how we'll react to a corporate decision. These predictions are based on previously captured data that was absorbed by the various senses. For example, pretend you're at the beach. You feel the cool breeze whisk across your face and the sand between your toes as you walk along the shore. You hear the cawing of seagulls and the waves crashing against the rocks. You see the magnificent sunset and a sailboat heeling into the wind. You taste sea salt and smell the freshness of the air. As you continue to walk, you feel something between your toes other than sand. It's solid. Is it a crab or a pearl shell? Your neocortex kicks in and makes a prediction while creating a memory based on the outcome of your new experience.

The four lobes of the neocortex perform different functions (Figure 1-1):

- The *frontal lobe* enables cognitive thinking and controls functions such as judgment, speech, and reasoning.

- The *parietal lobe* controls tactile sensory information and spatial relations.

- The *temporal lobe* concerns memory, hearing, sequencing, and organization.

- The *occipital lobe* interprets visual information.

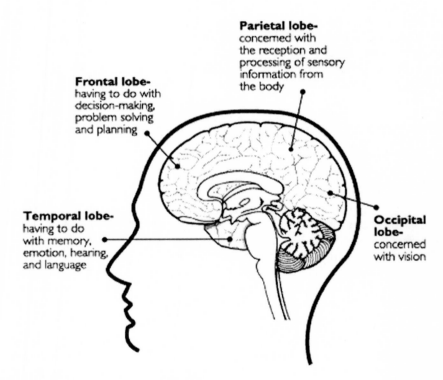

Parietal lobe- concerned with the reception and processing of sensory information from the body

Frontal lobe- having to do with decision-making, problem solving and planning

Temporal lobe- having to do with memory, emotion, hearing, and language

Occipital lobe- concerned with vision

Figure 1-1. The four lobes of the neocortex[1]

[1]"Brain Anatomy," http://teens.drugabuse.gov/educators/curricula-and-lesson-plans/mind-over-matter/mom-teachers-guide/brain-anatomy, last modified June 26, 2013.

I will focus on the frontal lobe because it is concerned with executing certain behaviors that correspond to the core functions of any business executive, including decision making, problem solving, planning, creating, speculating, learning, concentrating, focusing, awareness, attention, observation, and consciousness. The frontal lobe is what enables you to hypothesize about opportunities; instigate; make conscious decisions; control spontaneous, impulsive, and emotional social and sexual behaviors; and learn new things. The frontal lobe includes the following subregions, among others:

- The *prefrontal cortex* is fundamental to the performance of skills that need intelligence. It enables high-level planning.

- The *orbitofrontal cortex* is a part of the prefrontal cortex that is essential for risk and reward assessment as well as moral judgment.

- The *primary motor cortex* controls the muscles from the spinal cord.

- The *premotor cortex* consciously monitors movement sequences by using sensory feedback.

Of these several frontal lobe subregions, I will, again, focus on only one—the prefrontal cortex.

The prefrontal cortex is located just above your eyes behind your forehead. When you focus and concentrate hard, do you automatically rub your forehead? You're not alone. My mother does this all the time while she tries to recall something. Then she slaps her forehead when she remembers it!

The prefrontal cortex is what makes primates different from other species because it is where deeper or higher thinking occurs. It plays an important part in memory, conscious thinking, intellectual thoughts, concentration, cognitive analysis, motivation, creativity, emotions, and personality. This brain region gives you the capacity to exercise critical thinking and reasoning in social situations when presented with difficulty.

The prefrontal cortex—often referred to as the CEO, decision maker, or executive center of the brain—takes in information from all of the senses and arranges thoughts and actions to achieve specific goals. The main *executive functions* of the prefrontal cortex include the following:

- Concentrating

- Processing ideas and mental reactions in a way that lets you choose what to do next

- Predicting possible futures based on your present conduct or that of others

- Creating approaches ahead of time

- Making choices that consider both what you want now and in the long term
- Altering or fine-tuning conduct when circumstances shift
- Holding back on urges and waiting to get what you want
- Dialing back overly strong feelings
- Taking into account a variety of factors at the same time while dealing with new, sometimes difficult material

Controlled Consciousness

As you read this book, try to be in a controlled conscious state of mind. That is, be fully aware of yourself internally by directing your attention to your breathing, your sensations, and your heartbeat, among other things. This awareness will result in a form of "deliberate consciousness," which will alter the frequency of your brain waves, taking them from a heightened, intense state of alertness.

Uncontrolled consciousness, on the other hand, is activated by fear and anxiety. It can negatively influence both individual and organizational thoughts and actions. For example, if a company experiences a crisis like a security data breach, employees' antennas instantly go up but in a chaotic, reactive manner. Paranoia and panic combined with feelings of stress, anxiety, and confusion make it more difficult to problem solve and make good decisions. These same feelings often cloud work performance under any situation.

Let's do a brief consciousness-raising exercise. What emotions are you feeling right now? How deep is your breathing? How fast is your heart beating? Is there chatter going on in your mind? If so, bring your focus back to your breathing. Pay attention to the changes in your current emotional state and physical well-being. Are you feeling more relaxed? How is your posture? Are your breaths becoming stronger and deeper?

As you become aware of your inner self, notice what is happening to your body and your mind. As you pass oxygen into your brain, you will notice that your attention becomes more focused, which causes you to be more aware. This is the state I want you in as you read this book.

The Business Mind

You've probably heard someone say, "So-and-so has a real mind for business." Think about what that means. How is a business mind different from a non-business mind? A business mind doesn't just do what it is taught and told to do. A business mind is an innovative, self-aware mind marked by the syndrome of characteristics in Chart 1-1.

Chart 1-1. Characteristics of the Business Mind

Inspires	Looks for teamwork, not credit	Motivates others
Mentors	Respects and empowers others; is caring and compassionate	Surrounds itself with successful people
Ambitious	Thinks ahead of the competition	Has a purpose, mission, goal, and intention; seeks fulfillment, not just in work, but in life
Observant	Wants others to succeed and excel	Looks to help others
Creative	Merges applications and processes	Maintains health, family, wellness, and lifestyle balance
Committed	Analyzes and thinks outside the box	Shares information
Takes action	Stays connected with positive people	Knows how to make the right business decisions
Approachable	Engages others in interactive dialogue	Has leadership skills
Innovative	Changes the way business is conducted	Comfortable with themselves and surroundings
Confident	Uses technology to maximum advantage	Is confident in the data and information accessed
Welcomes ideas	Risks and invests in themselves and others	Prioritizes and knows which steps and actions to take next
Acknowledges others	Steps out of their comfort zone to make change happen	Able to communicate and speak at a level that makes sense to everyone
Gets to the root cause	Pursues mentors, coaches, and trainers and is always learning	Keeps a personal improvement journal detailing obstacles and successes
Embraces competition	Helps employees and peers get organized and succeed	Recognizes opportunities
Has analytical reasoning	Is proactive and persistent	Gets access to data faster
Collaborates with others	Controls the situation and takes responsibility and accountability	Transforms the business

As you looked at the chart, could you relate to all of the characteristics? If so, then congratulations, you have a business mind. If not, congratulations are also in order as you've recognized what you need to work on.

Purpose and the Business Mind

You can easily tell when someone has a business mind. Someone who has their business mind switched to "on" typically works with passion and purpose. They are fully present and love their work. The people they engage with experience the full joy that radiates from them. Their ebullient, positive energy is captivating. They are finding deep pleasure in their business and life. They are in harmony with themselves and their surroundings.

People with a business mind also possess long-term as well as short-term vision. They set their goals higher and desire bigger outcomes. Many think that bigger outcomes always equate with money, but upon diving deeper, it usually turns out this is not the reason.

For example, my personal purpose is to spend quality time with my grandparents and mother; to visit my brother when and for how long I desire; to work with programs that help support those with mental disabilities and disease; to empower future generations; to travel the world; to passionately dance; to share smiles and laughter with those who cross my path; to uplift, motivate, and inspire many; and to resonate love and compassion.

To fulfill my purpose, I realized I needed money, but I also knew that I needed to make some conscious changes. They weren't easy and didn't happen overnight, but eventually I decluttered and simplified my business. I moved my company to the cloud, so I could work where and when I chose.

I now feel more focused and much healthier and happier with where I am in my life. I now have more time to do the things I really love to do. I get to help people change their lives and businesses. This book, in fact, fulfills part of my purpose to make a difference and create new opportunities for others.

Keep in mind that you can have multiple purposes, which can evolve and change over time. Just make sure that whatever your purpose is, you are conscious of it every day and dedicate at least some of your activities to meeting your goals.

Purpose and Your Company's Mission

Just as an individual needs a purpose, an organization needs one too. Your company's mission statement should reflect its purpose and ideal current state. The values of a company are its core principles. The vision statement should portray the vision for tomorrow. Can you instantly recall your company's mission, values, and vision? If you have to look them up, then you are not consciously working in the spirit of your company's mission.

If you could, would you refine it? If so, what would it be? These are crucial questions everyone in your organization must ask themselves to achieve their full potential.

As an example, the following are the mission, values, and vision of the US Department of Agriculture (USDA):

Mission

We provide leadership on food, agriculture, natural resources, rural development, nutrition, and related issues based on sound public policy, the best available science, and efficient management.[2]

Values

Transparency — Making the Department's management processes more open so that the public can learn how USDA supports Americans every day in every way.

Participation — Providing opportunities for USDA constituents to shape and improve services provided by the Department.

Collaboration — Working cooperatively at all governmental levels domestically and internationally on policy matters affecting a broad audience.

Accountability — Ensuring that the performance of all employees is measured against the achievement of the Department's strategic goals.

Customer Focus — Serving USDA's constituents by delivering programs that address their diverse needs.

Professionalism — Building and maintaining a highly skilled, diverse, and compassionate workforce.

Results Orientation — Measuring performance and making management decisions to direct resources to where they are used most effectively.[3]

Vision

To expand economic opportunity through innovation, helping rural America to thrive; to promote agriculture production sustainability that better nourishes Americans while also helping feed others throughout the world; and to preserve and conserve our Nation's natural resources through restored forests, improved watersheds, and healthy private working lands.

---

[2]"Mission Statement United States Department of Agriculture (USDA)," www.usda.gov/wps/portal/usda/usdahome?navid=MISSION_STATEMENT, last modified on February 25, 2013.
[3]"Strategic Plan United States Department of Agriculture (USDA)," www.ocfo.usda.gov/usdasp/sp2010/sp2010.pdf, accessed on June 29, 2013.

The following is the mission statement for Food and Nutrition Service (FNS), one of USDA's subagencies[4]:

To increase food security and reduce hunger in partnership with cooperating organizations by providing children and low income people access to food, a healthful diet, and nutrition education in a manner that supports American agriculture and inspires public confidence.

An internal USDA department, the Office of Inspector General (OIG), has its own mission, values, and vision statement[5]:

Mission

OIG's mission is to promote economy, efficiency, effectiveness, and integrity in the delivery of USDA's programs.

Values

We place value on people. We earn and give respect to everyone we encounter in our work. We treat our fellow OIG team members as equal partners and full contributors to OIG's mission, vision, and goals.

We place value on making a positive difference through the work we do. We are committed to constantly improving how we operate, embracing innovation, and using persistence and determination to achieve results.

Vision

OIG will be a trusted contributor to the value, safety, and integrity of USDA programs.

The point of showing you these various samples is to illustrate that an organization can have multiple missions, values, and visions as long as they fulfill the same ultimate purpose. This can be accomplished by working with the Four Transformational Intelligences.

Likewise, a company's business goals, objectives, and initiatives should align with the company's mission, values, and vision. The following illustration, in Figure 1-2, shows the USDA's strategic plan for 2010-2015 with results for how FNS met one of USDA's goals in 2013.

---

[4]"Food and Nutrition Service (FNS) FY 2013 Strategic Priorities," www.fns.usda.gov/fns/about/FY2013-priorities.pdf, accessed on June 29, 2013.
[5]"U.S. Department of Agriculture Office of Inspector General Five-Year Strategic Plan Fiscal Years 2010-2015," www.usda.gov/oig/webdocs/OIGStrat2010-2015_508.pdf, accessed on July 1, 2013.

Goal	Objectives	Initiatives
USDA's Goal #4 - Ensure that All of America's Children Have Access to Safe, Nutritious and Balanced Meals	FNS Objective 4.1: Increase Access to Nutritious Food	Improve Access to Nutrition Assistance: Raise awareness and improving understanding of eligibility requirements to ensure eligible people, can access program benefits for which they are eligible easily and with dignity and respect.
		Improve Program Integrity: Maintain public confidence and good stewardship through efficient program delivery, strong customer service, and reduced improper payments.
	FNS Objective 4.2: Promote Healthy Diet and Physical Activity Behaviors	Improve Nutrition: Improve the food served in schools and child care centers, and promote healthful choices in SNAP and other nutrition assistance programs, to support healthier choices and promote better health.

Figure 1-2. FNS meeting USDA goal #4 for 2013

Goals are guidelines that lay out what you want to achieve. They are generally long-term in nature and usually represent broad visions (such as "safe, nutritious, and balanced meals").

Objectives define strategies or implementation steps to attain the identified goals (such as "increase access to nutritious food"). Objectives are specific, measurable, and have a defined completion date ("2013" for FNS). They are more specific and outline the *who, what, when, where,* and *how* of reaching the goals.

Initiatives are the tasks or day-to-day activities (such as "strong customer service") that allow the objective to be effective and goals to be accomplished.

Controlled Focus

Your conscious mind, as powerful as it is, can focus on and retain information for approximately ten seconds or less. So you must consciously decide where you direct your focus. How do you control it? By choice. You *choose* what to focus on. You *decide* what thoughts and what kind of thinking you allow into your mind.

As mentioned at the beginning of this chapter, the conscious mind is the part of the brain that performs critical thinking, reasoning, goal setting, and planning. The subconscious mind, where beliefs, habits, and actions exist, is what causes us to execute and take action. If we apply this to a company structure, the CEO is the equivalent to the conscious part of the brain. He or she gives orders, makes decisions, plans, and directs the company on what to do. The executives reporting to the CEO symbolize the subconscious.

For example, if your company has a meeting automatically scheduled every week on the same day, at the same time, at the same location, and with the same agenda, your staff's subconscious will kick in and they will go on autopilot. The staff begins to predict what will happen in the meeting. These predictions are drawn from memory, which is stored in the subconscious. The meeting becomes an uncontrolled habit of actions as illustrated in Figure 1-3.

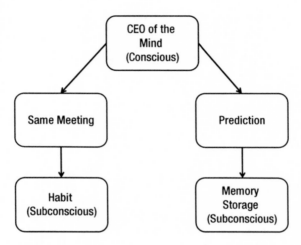

Figure 1-3. CEO of the mind

Let's say that one day, however, the CEO announces the meeting will be held on a bus on a Sunday, not a regular workday. This disorients the minds of the team. Their conscious awareness is focused and on full alert because it is no longer able to draw from past experience.

The CEO has the control to create new habits, to change the expectations of information needed in the meetings, and to shift the mind to form new actions.

The Four Transformational Intelligences and Change

What kind of CEO are you? Do you have the will to make something happen or do you believe you are powerless over certain situations? Since any type of change is hard, strong determination and full consciousness on your part are absolutely imperative to succeed.

The Four Transformational Intelligences will guide you through change. As shown in Figure 1-4, the Four Transformational Intelligences paint a picture of how your mindset should be as you start out on your journey.

Financial Intelligence	Reinvest and Regrow how you exceed revenue capacity
Customer Intelligence	Rethink and Redefine how you attract and maintain customers
Data Intelligence	Reinvent and Recreate the way you see, organize, collaborate, and interpret information
Mastermind Intelligence	Rewire the way your company communicates, operates, solves problems, interacts, creates, and innovates

Figure 1-4. The Four Transformational Intelligences

Chapters 2–5 explore each of the Four Intelligences in turn. Chapters 6 and 7 show where you can make changes most effectively in your organization based on pattern recognition and strategy mapping practices.

The overarching purpose of the processes you will be learning is to help you make critical decisions to transform your company and drive value. You need to consistently ask yourself two questions:

- How confident am I that my organization's performance will improve?

- Why should I believe the information I have before me is accurate?

Most executives and decision makers struggle to answer these two questions. This book provides you with the framework for unlocking the answers to them. Once you understand this framework, you will be able to apply it to make decisions and take action that will drive transformation and improve collaboration and communication across your organization.

My goal is not to give you all the knowledge you will ever need to approach change, but rather to open your mind to opportunities, get you excited about the possibilities, to have breakthroughs and "a-ha" moments, and to motivate you enough to consistently apply the exercises in this book, so that the approach becomes a part of your subconscious.

The best way to begin to implement the Four Transformational Intelligences is to identify a central controlled area within your business that can make an impact and cause a ripple effect. For example, the legal department within an organization touches all other departments and can serve as a controlled area where you could apply a systematic approach.

During this process, I encourage you to make note of where changes can be applied specifically to your business. Since your business mind will be turned on, focused, and consciously aware, use a journal, notepad, smartphone, or tablet to jot down your thoughts as you go.

Once you understand how to implement the Four Transformational Intelligences, you will gain clarity and confidence. After you internalize the framework, you will easily and intuitively be able to apply this newfound lens to meet unforeseen changes and changing business environments proactively, strategically, and with a sense of purpose.

And now, on to change.

Financial Intelligence

Reinvest in Yourself and Your Business

*The test of a first-rate intelligence is the ability to hold two opposed ideas
in mind at the same time and still retain the ability to function.*

— F. Scott Fitzgerald

Financial Intelligence, which I also call *Financial Transformational Intelligence*, uti-
lizes special strategies and certain aspects of brain biology to optimize the
insights you generate while looking at your organization's financial data. This
approach, which also quiets the unconscious patterns of thinking that keep
you from seeing as clearly as possible, helps you see new opportunities, which
lead to new decisions. You can then create new initiatives that align with your
organization's mission, strategic goals, and objectives.

Neuroeconomics

Our brains are wired with certain circuits and chemical reactions that are
based on how we capture and process information. Each time we are faced
with triggers such as stress or pressure, our brain releases chemicals and
refers to known pathways in order to make a decision. Do I save or spend?
Should I invest or sell? If I give, will I gain anything in return?

Most business people act based on automatic, chemical reactions that keep them from responding to the information they have with a clear perspective. It's as if their brain's software is making rote, habitual decisions for them. But if you understand how the software works, you can reprogram it to see the bigger picture.

There is a whole new field of study based on the advances made in understanding what happens in the brain when humans make business decisions. It's called *neuroeconomics*, and it has become important in the last decade. Degrees in neuroeconomics are now offered by universities that include MIT, Harvard, Yale, Carnegie Mellon, Princeton, and George Mason. To understand the breadth of this subject, all you have to do is look at a description of the Center for Neuroeconomics Studies (CNS) at Claremont Graduate University, which says that researchers "draw on economic theory, experimental economics, neuroscience, endocrinology, and psychology to develop a comprehensive understanding of human decisions."[1]

Trust, Fear, and Reward

Let's start by focusing on three emotional responses—trust, fear, and reward. When these responses are encountered during business activities, they trigger an associated neurological action in executives and decision makers.

Trust

Trust comes in different forms. Perhaps you trust in the data you have in front of you. Maybe you trust in the people who provided you with that information. Hopefully, you trust in yourself to make correct and impactful decisions.

What is your experience with trust? Do you trust until proven wrong or do you question until trust is gained? What is your comfort level when it comes to trust?

The next time you are handed a report, examine your reaction to the trust you have in that report—including both the data and the human interaction aspects of your reaction. How much do you "love" the report?

According to Dr. Paul J. Zak, founding director of CNS, love is the foundation of trust. But what does love have to do with economics and financial decisions, let alone a report?

---

[1] Center for Neuroeconomics Studies, "Center for Neuroeconomics Studies," www.neuroeconomicstudies.org, accessed on August 5, 2013.

If you like investing, you probably follow an analyst that you trust in the market. Maybe you read his blogs, pay attention to their latest trending thoughts on Twitter, and even follow the influencers who they follow. Focus and think about this person for a few seconds. If you really can't think of an analyst, try picturing a coach, mentor, public figure, or even a celebrity who inspires you. Would you trust him enough to give him your money to invest with? Why do you feel connected to them? Did one of your friends or colleagues influence you to feel positively about this individual?

When you relate to a person, event, or even a piece of writing, you tend to feel safe and connected, which creates a feeling of trust. Trust triggers the release of oxytocin, commonly known as the "love hormone." Oxytocin is released during childbirth, breastfeeding, and orgasms, as well as from the social bond humans have with other humans. Oxytocin is produced in the hypothalamus of the brain, as shown in Figure 2-1.

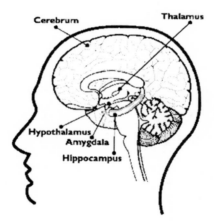

Figure 2-1. Location of the hypothalamus, where oxytocin is produced[2]

So how does this relate to neuroeconomics and business decisions? When we decide to trust someone or something, the bonding feeling we experience in the present is based on an association with a positive experience in our past, whether we consciously remember it or not. Often, due to information overload or pressure to make judgments too quickly, we make instant decisions based on trust, instinct, and a feeling of comfort, rather than through analysis of the issue in a stand-alone way. A thorough analysis will lead to better decisions.

---

[2]"Brain Anatomy," http://teens.drugabuse.gov/educators/curricula-and-lesson-plans/mind-over-matter/mom-teachers-guide/brain-anatomy, last modified June 26, 2013.

Fear

In business, we need to plan for potential losses and manage risks. These risks can be related to finance, security, legal issues, and data. Just reading the word "risk" can alter your thoughts and emotions, raise your pulse, and speed up your breathing. If that happened to you just now, it was because your brain was processing fear, worry, and uncertainty.

Risk is the potential to lose something when trying to gain something. Our reaction to loss is different than it is with risk. Loss is something you had that you are not able to recover.

Have you ever owned something that you took a huge loss on—either real estate, stocks, or something of sentimental value (an art collection) that broke or tore? Was it hard to let go? Did you hold onto it because you thought that the price might jump back up? Maybe you stored it away in the closet to figure out a way to repair it later. How did your pride and ego factor into your course of action? More than likely you spent time and money taking more risks trying to recover what you lost.

Generally, humans hate to lose, so when we suffer a loss, we sometimes take risks on top of risks in the hopes of recovering. This is usually a bad idea.

A major influence when it comes to risk and reward is "risk aversion."[3] For example, imagine you're a business owner and a situation arises where you have no choice but to choose another company to partner with. Company A has a guaranteed contract with a client valued at $1M. Company B has a 50% chance of closing with a $10M contract. Which do you choose? Even though Company A has a lower expected value, most decision makers prefer a guarantee. Would your decision change if the guaranteed contract from Company A was $500K instead of $1M?

Risk aversion is where decision makers give up expected value for a higher degree of certainty, even with a lower payoff. However, because of other non-monetary related factors—such as Company B's visibility in the market or Company B being known as a company that's easy to do business with—your decision might be based on expected utility instead of expected income.

Pay attention to what stimulates you to make certain choices in business when it comes to risk.

If the scenario is reversed from potential profit to potential loss, where Company A has a guaranteed loss of $1M vs. Company B's 50% chance of a $10M loss, what partnership would you decide to take? Most would choose

---

[3]Michael L. Platt and Scott A. Huettel. "Risky Business: the Neuroeconomics of Decision Making Under Certainty." *Nature Neuroscience*, April 2008; 11(4): 398–403, www.ncbi.nlm.nih.gov/pmc/articles/PMC3065064/#!po=65.3846.

Company B because there is a possibility, not a guarantee, that you won't lose anything even though the monetary value of loss could potentially be higher. This is known as "loss aversion," a term first coined by Daniel Kahneman and Amos Tversky.[4]

The adverse feelings that result from a definite loss can be deeper than the feelings from an uncertain risk. Typically the feeling that appears is fear or stress. In many cases, they're actually the same thing. Stress is often simply a milder form of fear. You experience stress because you are afraid that the outcome of a situation won't be optimal or you're afraid you won't get your needs met.

Fear of loss or risk releases chemicals and adrenaline to the body causing harmful results, mostly health issues. The signals that are sent to the brain cause one of three reactions: a flight, fight, or freeze response. During different situations of fear, one is more dominant than the other.

Think about investing in a new program within your company. It could be cloud computing, big data analytics, mergers and acquisitions, or any other big ticket item. At this point in time, if you're feeling fear, you are unconsciously re-imagining disasters from your past. We have all had disastrous moments. Maybe the projects were under-budgeted or required lots of rework due to failure. Maybe because of the failure, you disappointed stakeholders, customers, or partners. Whatever it was, you are unconsciously linking the present situation to that one.

Focus on your various fearful thoughts. What is your typical initial response when it comes to those frightening times? Typically it comes down to one of these three items:

- "Nothing is ever going to be the same. How do I face people?" - Flight response

- "Who is responsible for this mess?" - Fight response

- "I don't know what to do to get out of this mess." - Freeze response

In business, your reaction to fear might be different than in your personal life. For example, stressful business meetings cause my mind to react with a fight response. No, I don't jump across the table and strangle someone. Instead my mind starts to work like a puzzle to figure things out—fighting back with the stress.

However, in my romantic life, I used to be a runner. I wouldn't make it to the second date—usually fleeing, hiding, or running away. I feared something that hadn't even happened yet. Since I began the process of paying attention to

---

[4]Daniel Kahneman and Amos Tversky. "Choices, values, and frames." *American Psychologist*, Vol 39(4), April 1984; 39(4): 341–350, http://dx.doi.org/10.1037/0003-066X.39.4.341.

myself, I know how my mind works and I can ignore the initial fear and its automatic impulse to flee. I am in control of my mind. I have the power to decide what messages to send off in my brain.

When it comes to fear, your brain releases chemical messengers that influence your behavior. When you become conscious of these signals, you can alter behaviors and react differently to events. Fear is neither positive nor negative. Within the brain, the region responsible for fear and aggressive behavior is called the amygdala.[5] The amygdala reaches into the memory and retrieves warning signs related to fear—Caution! Careful! Danger! Fear can protect you by signaling to your brain about events such as the following:

- oncoming car - caution

- hot stove - careful

- shark in the water – there's danger

Recognize the types of fear messages that your body sends. Pay attention to your own mind. Your mind can be trained to overcome almost any fear, whether it is related to money, food, failure, relationships, or even flying.

The amygdala, shown in Figure 2-2, is the part of the brain that deals with emotions, learning, and memories relating to fear. Fear causes your mind to predict outcomes that have not occurred yet based on memories and emotions from the past. You can train your mind to learn to refocus on the positive, rewarding outcome that fear can bring instead of the negative.

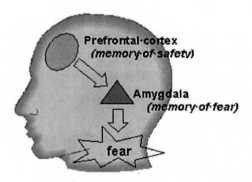

Figure 2-2. Amygdala and prefrontal cortex relationship[6]

---

[5]National Institute of Mental Health, "Brain Basics," www.nimh.nih.gov/health/educational-resources/brain-basics/brain-basics.shtml, accessed August 9, 2013.
[6]National Institute of Mental Health, "Mimicking Brain's 'All Clear' Quell's Fear in Rats." www.nih.gov/news/pr/nov2002/nimh-06.htm, accessed August 9, 2013.

As mentioned in Chapter 1, the prefrontal cortex of our brain, (responsible for decision-making, problem-solving, and judgment), has the ability to plan the course of actions based on signals received from the amygdala. In other words, after the initial emotional reaction of fear coming from the amygdala, the prefrontal cortex decides what reaction and course of action to take to get out of the fearful, stress-producing event. It is the prefrontal cortex that allows you to decide to take conscious control of your anxieties.

You have the power to alter your fear with reward.

Reward

Reward-seeking is different in males than in females. The male neurobiological behavior patterns find competition and conflict rewarding. I once had dinner with an executive who was highly competitive, a sign of high testosterone levels. How did I realize he was so competitive? He kept mentioning the year-to-date billion dollar revenue he had brought into his company. At first I thought he was trusting me by sharing with me his pride in how hard his department was working. Then he went on and on about how he figured out a way to gain and lead the market while throwing other guys under the bus. When I presented him with the idea of helping society by offering services and education to uplift his customers' businesses—in other words, creating a "win-win" solution, he was not interested. His interest was self-centered—winning over competition and playing the power game.

Dr. Zak has further proven that higher levels of testosterone decreases financial and nonfinancial generosity. Generosity is driven by feelings of trust and empathy. Therefore, those with high levels of testosterone ("alpha males") are distrusting and uncompassionate. These alpha males demand generosity from others.

On the other hand, the female brain, which produces estrogen, rewards the seeking of social connection. As a response to fear-based events such as conflict, the female brain searches for solutions. These solutions involve compromise, even if it results in letting go of something of importance. Searching for a solution involving social interaction triggers trust, which, as mentioned above, produces oxytocin. This "tend-and-befriend" process that is dominantly found in female brain patterns is rewarding.[7]

---

[7] N. R. Lighthall, M. Mather, M. A. Gorlick, "Acute Stress Increases Sex Differences in Risk Seeking in the Balloon Analogue Risk Task." (2009), PLoS ONE 4(7): e6002 (2009). doi: 10.1371/journal.pone.0006002, www.plosone.org/article/info%3Adoi%2F10.1371%2Fjournal.pone.0006002.

We see an increase in the number of women in executive leadership roles year after year. Business models have changed; there is a desire for more engagement, collaboration, social activities, and interaction internally as well as with customers and partners. The female brain naturally possesses the characteristics that create the values to which many companies aspire.

Male and female bonding in the workplace has allowed the two to learn from each other. In recent years, both males and females have demonstrated signs of compassion in the workplace. This not only benefits their organization but society as well.

Leaders also promote, encourage, and reward employees and partners to contribute by mentoring, volunteering, and donating. These "giving" types of activities present rewarding empathic emotional feelings for both the giver and the receiver. The feeling of trust itself is rewarding. The tendency to reward a feeling of trust kicks in when the trusting behavior is positively reinforced. For example, when you trust a charity enough to donate to it and then you receive evidence of positive results, you feel rewarded.

Connecting with others through trusting interactions creates oxytocin in the brain, which reduces stress and calms the mind. But what gets the mind motivated, excited, and stimulated? The subconscious mind is continually seeking pleasure and anticipating reward, regardless of whether that reward is for the short or long term. Some rewards found through research include food, water, sex, money, and drugs.

The motivation that occurs is not about the actual attainment of the reward, but the probability of achieving it. This seeking behavior of the mind releases a neurotransmitter called dopamine in the brain. When there is a challenging goal that you expect to achieve, a surge of dopamine is released, which motivates you with a sense of pleasure. This focus on the anticipated reward, as opposed to fear, is what creates the business mind.

Males and females generally tackle the challenge differently, with males working independently and females working collaboratively.

One of the most important tools you can use to access your business mind, as well as the business mind of everyone else you deal with, is to focus on the reward. Create "win-win" solutions for your company, customers, and partners. Think of scenarios that will help your mind connect to reward. When you can train your mind to seek rewarding responses instead of fear, the brain releases "feel good" hormones instead of stressful ones.

Remember, the thought of fearful events is a negative prediction about the future. Do you want to dread fear or anticipate reward? It is your choice. The business mind will pick the reward. Distant rewards still trigger reward signals in your brain and a sense of contentment even if you know that the reward is long term. That is why a business mind aligns its financial goals to reward, and this is how Financial Intelligence blossoms.

Financial Intelligence

Don't think that Financial Intelligence only involves the chief financial officer (CFO), the finance department, or the financial lead within a nonfinance department. Financial Intelligence is for those involved with the organization's strategic goals, objectives, and initiatives. This should mean everyone.

Your task is to measure financial success—the impact a proposed activity will have on the company's performance by mapping and wiring your business mind to the strategic objective at hand. These objectives can include the following:

- Decreasing cost
- Increasing quality
- Increasing productivity
- Mergers and acquisitions
- Increasing growth (revenue, profits)
- Return on investments (ROI)
- Adding market share
- Optimizing cash flow
- Increasing profitability

You define the success.

You also define the reward. Reward is personal. It must have that "feel good" emotion attached. Remember, an anticipated reward motivates, excites, and stimulates an individual.

Not everyone views rewards in the same way. Maybe you want a yacht, a second home in a foreign country, or vacation time to spend with your family. You get to define what is rewarding for you. Here are some examples of different types of financial rewards:

- Bonuses
- Incentives
- Promotions
- Paid time off
- Paid vacations
- Supporting causes
- Additional benefits

- Recognitions and awards
- Living a healthy lifestyle
- Achieving your personal purpose
- Meeting the mission of the company

Financial Intelligence allows you to be consciously aware of the automatic analytical and intuitive processes of the brain, so you can train your mind to get out of your own way. It lets you override those processes that negatively affect performance while you focus on those that enhance it. Financial Intelligence combines analytics and intuition, where intuition is the awareness of the emotional feeling and brain activities that occur when evaluating the analytics. This results in intelligent decisions.

It is important with Financial Intelligence, as it is with all the other Intelligences, to collaborate and communicate. Input from other team members and departments is crucial and invaluable. The marketing department will have insight that the IT department might not have considered. That insight might trigger an issue that HR and legal need to address. For example, if the marketing department needs the IT department's help to track the correlation of employee and customer "likes" on social media, both the HR and legal department might wave a red flag about potential privacy law issues.

Let's pretend you're looking to reduce IT cost. Are you communicating and using your business mind to understand the other departments? What about understanding your IT support center? What are the types of incidents they are receiving? Is it a user training issue? Or are they supporting too many user products? Or are the version releases for each user too overwhelming to be supported?

There are many ways you can simultaneously work toward your company's mission while seeking financial success and personal reward. Just look at the big business picture. Take into account the many factors that can and are impacting your business. These factors include the economy, legislative mandates and regulations, customer and partner needs, technology implementations, and of course your competition.

Next, we'll look at a few subcategories of Financial Intelligence: Predictive Intelligence, Risk Intelligence, and Business Intelligence.

Predictive Intelligence

The CFO of an organization needs to think about future investments. These investments could be in new tools, mergers and acquisitions, or employee productivity programs. At the same time, the CFO needs to evaluate the entire company's financial performance.

To predict future financial performance, a CFO needs to forecast trends based on the company's historical activity. The CFO requires financial analytics to drill down into the relationship of cause and effect to understand why incidents occur.

How can CFOs sift through enormous amounts of financial data, extract useful ones, and interpret the information to make actionable changes that make an impact? The answer is Predictive Intelligence.

Predictive Intelligence is based on historical data and projections about the market. It is mostly about estimates and assumptions. When you are presenting numbers about a potential idea to an executive, guess what? They are based on estimates and assumptions.

A lack of collaboration or insight into other departments within an organization often leads to the omission of certain useful financial numbers. These numbers are important when executives need to make decisions based on the overall health of the company.

For example, let's take marketing and outreach activities. The investments made in these areas, like all other investments, are based on estimates and assumptions of how much our company will benefit based on these initiatives. We assume data from the past will help us with our prediction about the future. There's no guarantee, however, of that being true.

Risk Intelligence

Measuring risk is about making predictions. As we noted, Predictive Intelligence makes estimates and assumptions based on historical data and/or experience. With Risk Intelligence, we are making estimates and assumptions about the risk of a future event. It is about understanding the amount of risk you and your organization are willing to take.

Earlier we uncovered risk aversion, which has to do with influential decisions about risks and rewards. Here we dive a bit deeper for you to get comfortable with risk. Risk Intelligence is about understanding when you start to get uncomfortable. Then you trust in your own discomfort to make innovative judgment calls. The idea is to determine a risk range that you can effectively tolerate and control.

You might have different comfort ranges for different types of risk. If you are running an international company, then you might have different risk tolerance for legislative mandates and regulations according to policies in different countries.

How much risk are you willing to bear and take? What is your attitude toward risk? What about non-monetary types of risk such as reputation?

Risks with a potential reward give the decision maker a greater appetite—unrewarded risks reduce the appetite for risk.

Keep in mind that circumstances will continually change and so will opportunities; therefore, you will need to readjust your risk range on a regular basis. How is risk viewed within your organization? Are you encouraging Risk Intelligence discussions to occur? Be honest and realistic with yourself and others in your business. Allow them to share their thoughts on risk. A true business mind seeks input from others. Understand their risk tolerance and how it stacks up to yours. You will need their buy-in for any strategy or action you take to be successful.

Business Intelligence

Within the industry, Business Intelligence has come to be known as a type of reporting tool. Here I refer to Business Intelligence as a transformational mindset, where you look from the outside in to see your business, from high up in the sky. Look at the good and bad, positive and negative impacts, internal and external concerns—I mean all of it. The Business Intelligence mindset is about asking "How do my initiatives support overall strategy?" when weighing future measures.

For example, if your company is running on an accrual basis of accounting, revenue is recorded when the transaction is completed. It is not when you receive final payment, but when the "consider it done" is actually accomplished.

Let's pretend you were part of a software company that ran on an accrual basis several years ago. Back then, software was shipped with separate key codes. Sometimes it would take two weeks just to deliver the package, so it took two weeks after a sale for revenue to be recordable. However, using your Business Intelligence and collaborating with your internal employees and external partners, you pushed yourself out of your comfort zone to deliver software instantaneously over the Internet.

A decision like this allowed your company to record revenue faster and more efficiently. You also saved money on tracking, manufacturing, and quality control. Additional savings were passed on to your distributors and resellers. Customers loved you because they could get their software right away. Heck, you even helped the environment.

You became a hero in your company and a star in your industry, just by moving out of your comfort zone of doing things the way they were usually done.

Sounds great, right?

Okay, I know. You weren't the one who invented instant downloadable software. But it happened to somebody. You would have needed to use the principles of Financial Intelligence to pull off such a massive change. There would have been a lot of Risk Intelligence required to estimate the costs and risks involved—and some courage—and perhaps a mastery of some risk aversion to pull this particular trigger.

If you follow the Financial Intelligence model with your business, you could be the next hero or heroine.

Now let's look at an issue from today's world—the issue of maintenance that is offered with yearly IT support services. In the realm of accrual accounting, those one-year support services have not been "delivered" yet. If it takes a full year before they are considered "delivered," how are they accounted for? (For professional services, the work must be completed before the revenue from it can be recognized.)

Different business models recognize earned revenue differently.

Now that cloud computing allows for month-to-month pricing models, how is that revenue entered into the accounting system? What financial adjustments need to be made—pertaining not only to the booking of the sale, but also to other relevant internal and external processes, customers, distributors, resellers, and partners offering complementary services. Many cloud computing business models are able to record offerings as unearned income due to the prepaid quarterly or yearly pricing models, which allows for working capital. This is a completely different way of looking at the same accounting issue.

My goal here is not to provide accounting advice, but to help you stay alert to the possibility of constant improvement to financial success by using your Business Intelligence mindset. Using that mindset, you have the potential to alter your business model and improve your organization's finances.

We all know that there are certain kinds of financial risks that need to be justified, whatever your business model. However, financial and accounting professionals should not be the only ones making financial decisions for the company. Collaborative involvement of executives and other company decision makers is crucial in order to adopt a Business Intelligence mindset and shift the business model.

Don't be afraid to evolve. Sometimes you have to create new business models. And guess what? Successful businesses can't survive using the same routine. Why? Factors surrounding them are in constant motion. Imagine waking up every day and everything is exactly the same. The days repeat themselves, over and over. How boring! Instead of dreading change, invite it in. Embrace competition. Anticipate unexpected rewards. Some amazing things might actually happen. You might not only shift your company into something new and exciting, but create a positive and rewarding movement in society.

Re-Purpose

Often an executive needs to give new meaning and life to a business. It could be because of flat or decreasing profits or new competition, or because the market has changed somehow. Re-purposing comes in the form of new activities in business areas like marketing or research and development. The executive may also explore new industry innovations or establish new employee programs that will help ensure the survival of the business.

A recent example of re-purposing comes from the public sector. Mr. Curtis (Curt) L. Coy, Deputy Under Secretary for Economic Opportunity for the Department of Veterans Affairs (VA), was recently challenged to re-purpose his department when the Veterans Retraining Assistance Program (VRAP) act went into effect.[8]

On November 21, 2011, in the Eisenhower Executive Office Building South Court Auditorium, US President Barack Obama signed the VOW to Hire Heroes Act.[9] This bipartisan bill passed by Congress provides tax benefits to businesses that not only hire veterans, but also provide them with education and training opportunities. Within the act, a new law offers unemployed veterans up to 12 months of training assistance.

Mr. Coy, a disabled veteran, was responsible for vocational rehabilitation and employment within the department. He was given no additional funds or resources to create this new training program, which needed to be in place within seven and a half months from the date the president signed the bill.

The new training program, slated to begin on July 1, 2012, was designed for unemployed veterans between the ages of 35 and 60 who had no education benefits. The program was to accept 99,000 applications until September 30, 2013. "If you stand back and look at the Department of Labor, Bureau of Labor Statistics' data, there are about 800,000 unemployed veterans. About half of them are between the ages of 35 to 60," said Coy, ". . . we needed to . . . convince 99,000 of them, or 25%, to attend school full-time for a year to use these benefits."

Mr. Coy was now faced with operational and marketing issues to solve. The first was "putting together the program, in other words, how do you accept the applications, how do you review them, how do you notify the veteran, how do you start paying the benefits, and so on." The second was setting up the outreach. "You can do this whole process piece," he said, "and if nobody applies [to the program] then the process piece doesn't work."

---

[8]Curtis (Curt) L. Coy. Interview by author. Face-to-face/tape recording. Selbyville, DE, August 18, 2013. The opinions are those of Mr. Curtis Coy—not necessarily those of Congress or of the president of the United States.

[9]United States Department of Veterans Affairs, "VOW to Hire Heroes Act 2011, " http://benefits.va.gov/vow/index.htm, accessed August 18, 2013.

Mr. Coy, like many other executives working in complex enterprise environments, was tasked with reinvesting in and regrowing his business. When an existing business adopts a new program initiative, executives need to strategically and tactically plan. The plan could include reallocation of resources, repositioning of funds, or evaluating and altering schedules (or other criteria) of current programs already in place. This activity is the re-purposing we've been discussing in this chapter.

Mr. Coy had to re-purpose with no additional funds and approximately 20,000 existing staff members by applying a Financial Intelligence business mind and focusing on the reward the program's outcome would generate.

"One of the good things about working at the Department of VA is that almost all its employees are really focused on knowing what the prime mission is—and that is to take care of veterans. They consider it an honor and privilege to do that. Sure you might get some folks with the initial eyeball rolls of 'we have more to do'—but they know what the end purpose and goal is and, as a result, they say, 'Thank you very much for this additional work.'"

That's what happens when you re-purpose. Everyone comes together to make a big change work.

Lather, Rinse, Repeat

Start small and make big impacts. Break it up into iterative cycles. You'll be doing this process over and over again, each time starting from a fresh place. You can also start the process from the viewpoint of different departments.

To stimulate your mind, focus on the rewards that are important to you and also to your colleagues, your team, your society, and especially your customers.

Financial Intelligence is deeply connected to your customers and their desires and values—which is what the next chapter on Customer Intelligence is all about.

Customer Intelligence

Redefine Your Business

All intelligent thoughts have already been thought; what is necessary is only to try to think them again.

— Johann Wolfgang von Goethe

Who are your customers? What are ways to attract them? When are you able to make that connection with them? Where can you find them? How do you reach them?

Answering these questions is the first part of Customer Intelligence. The second part of it deals with making sure all the departments within your organization share the same definition of their ideal customer. We'll get to that later in the chapter.

First, let's look at the latest brain-related marketing science that can help you attract new customers.

Neuromarketing

What part of the brain lights up when a customer decides, "Yes! I am buying that?" In recent years, neuroscientists have been studying consumers to determine how their brain reacts to different marketing activities, such as the package appeal,[1] product smell, influence of taste,[2] or response to advertisements. The practical application of neuroscientists' marketing research is called neuromarketing. There have been fascinating neuromarketing studies done around branding, lead generation, and selling.

The neuromarketing topics that are the most germane to Customer Intelligence are these two:

- What attracts customers?
- Why do customers come back for more?

Instant vs. Delayed Gratification for Customers

The thing that draws your customers in is the same thing that draws you in as a consumer: reward. As we learned in the last chapter, seeking rewards is what motivates, excites, and stimulates us.

But which is better: short-term rewards or long-term ones?

Studies have shown that customers seek instant gratification over delayed rewards.[3]

Not so long ago, we would patiently wait for reward certificates to come in the mail after spending the requisite amount at stores like DSW, Pier 1, and others. This is an example of delayed rewards.

Then, some retailers had the bright idea to offer instant in-store rewards without making us wait for them in the mail. Now we expect that from other stores and are disappointed when they can't satisfy our need for instant gratification.

Incentivizing Business Partners

But what about our business partners? Do we try to understand and treat partners the same way we do our customers? After all, aren't our partners a

---

[1]Laura N. Van der Laan, Denise T. D. De Ridder, Max A. Viergever, Paul A. M. Smeets, (2012) "Appearance Matters: Neural Correlates of Food Choice and Packaging Aesthetics," PLoS ONE 7(7):e41738. doi:10.1371/journal.pone.0041738.
[2]Simone Kühn and Jürgen Gallinat, (2013) "Does Taste Matter? How Anticipation of Cola Brands Influences Gustatory Processing in the Brain," PLoS ONE 8(4):e61569. doi:10.1371/journal.pone.0061569.
[3]Jeffrey Stevens, "Intertemporal Choice," *Encyclopedia of Animal Behavior*, edited by Michael D. Breed and Janice Moore. Amsterdam: Elsevier B.V., 2010, vol. 2, pp. 203-208, http://digitalcommons.unl.edu/cgi/viewcontent.cgi?article=1519&context=psychfacpub.

second-tier connection to our customers? They have the relationship and access we need. How are we rewarding our partners? Are we offering them instant or delayed gratification?

You depend on your partners to be your extra feet on the street, promoting and selling your brand, with high expectations to deliver. But are you rewarding them with instant or delayed gratification? Do you take into account their own cost of resources—employees, sales documentation, proposals—when compensating them? In essence, are you attracting or driving them away?

I am often asked, "What drives partners away?"

Here is a perfect example. Consider the payment terms you may have with a partner. Are they favorable, or is your partner often not paid until 60 days after the end of a specific quarter? Depending on many factors, it could take a few months before payment is received. This can be demotivating.

If partners don't see or feel instant satisfaction, then they may become disincentivized to work as hard as they can for your business. This might be their attitude: "If it comes, it comes. Why chase opportunities? I'll look for another partner." Companies will often spend a great deal of time and money to attract partners, but then lose them in the day-to-day interactions. Partners, like customers, seek immediate rewards.[4] They won't remain interested in the opportunity to work with you for long if all you offer them are the promise of rewards that take place in the future.

However, businesses need to be savvy in assessing their partners' satisfaction level. Satisfied partners, as well as customers, may be more likely to wait for a delayed reward if its value is significantly higher than the instant reward they crave.[5]

On the other hand, dissatisfied customers and partners prefer immediate results. Because of this, businesses need to come up with a middle ground to please both satisfied and dissatisfied partners. The idea is to offer both a small instant reward and a delayed one of higher value. One example of this is how students view the experience of obtaining a master's degree. There are smaller immediate rewards, such as positive feedback on papers and semester grades. The conferral of the actual degree represents the delayed reward that offers higher value satisfaction.

---

[4]Garret O' Connell, Anastasia Christakou, Anthony T. Haffey, Bhismadev Chakrabarti, (2013) "The Role of Empathy in Choosing Rewards from Another's Perspective." *Front. Hum. Neurosci.* 7:174, doi: 10.3389/fnhum.2013.00174.
[5]Melissa A. Z. Knoll, (2010) "The Role of Behavioral Economics and Behavioral Decision Making in Americans' Retirement Savings Decisions," Social Security Bulletin, vol. 70, no. 4, www.ssa.gov/policy/docs/ssb/v70n4/v70n4p1.html.

Depending on your industry and business model, partnership agreements can satisfy both instant and delayed rewards. Here are two possible examples:

- Offer a partner a small sign-on advance, followed by a higher, delayed royalty later on. This is similar to the arrangement that record companies use with their artists.

- Provide a small instant setup fee with a long-term greater margin value, which is often how product distribution agreements work.

There are pros and cons that should be carefully evaluated with every reward, whether it's instant or delayed. If you have a business model where partners compete against each other, be cautious about your setup. A manufacturer offering additional incentives (rebates or prizes) to the winning team may be incentivizing the wrong thing. These additional incentives might be more appealing, even though there is a delayed gratification. One of the partners might practically give away the sale to gain the additional incentives, which may have a negative effect on the perceived value of your product.

Then there are those who thrive on competition, who have a blood thirst for winning. They may defer immediate rewards in anticipation of the higher-valued delayed gratification. The planning and effort that go into winning the competition serves as their immediate reward—and it means more to them than any other short-term incentive you could offer.

Having a cut-throat competitor with tremendous drive who takes an instant lead in your competition can be a detriment to your remaining partners. The losing teams may lose interest because they won't be getting a long-term reward. This behavior will eventually put a dent in the cost of doing business with the competing partners who lose. They will look to do business with someone who will guarantee them rewards (instant and/or delayed). Table 3-1 demonstrates that in this scenario the losing partners not only lost an immediate reward, but lost a delayed one as well.

Table 3-1. Manufacturer Losing Partnerships Due to Competitive Business Model

Manufacturer Competitive Business Model with Partners					
Competitor	Markup to Resell to Customer	Status	Award	Reward	End Result
#1	1%	Lost	No Immediate Award	No Delayed Award	Find Other Business Partner
#2	0%	Won	Immediate Award – 0%	Future Incentive (Rebates, Prize)	Continue Doing Business
#3	2%	Lost	No Immediate Award	No Delayed Award	Find Other Business Partner

It is amazing how many times business decision makers think of opportunities to engage partners, spend lots of money to attract them, and then question why partners are not doing business with them anymore. A well thought-out intelligence plan was not applied.

Just as some partners may decide it is not worthwhile to do business with you, you may also decide that it's time to abandon certain partners. Business partners can impact your business positively or negatively and can affect everything from your bottom line to your reputation. As such, you must constantly evaluate the state of your partner relationships.

I once had an executive of a major corporation tell me I would go bankrupt if I partnered with his company. Apparently, he didn't want to change his business model to conform to the needs of his partners. He did me a huge favor by being candid, because he had a point. He was not the kind of executive I wanted to do business with. If his company was in a position to have a partner go bankrupt, then his company had an issue that he should have done something about.

Partners are not the only ones you may need to step away from. Evaluate your customers. Is it rewarding to do business with them? What kind of reward are you seeking—instant, delayed, or both? Just like service companies go through a bid/no-bid evaluation process to decide if they will pursue an opportunity, so should you.

On a grander scale, let's look at the business of contracting for the government. Many businesses are hesitant to get involved with the government even on a small scale. Why is that?

Once again, it comes down to rewards. Doing business with the government doesn't produce an immediate reward. It results in a high-value, delayed gratification, which many businesses find risky. The reward is great, but it will be received in the distant future.

As a business owner who does business with the government, let me give you an example of what it's like. After a series of meetings, phone calls, and e-mails with a particular department or agency, your team devises a viable solution for the issue at hand, then works extensively on an exhaustive and lengthy proposal. After months of anticipation, you hear back from the contracting officer who begins the negotiation process. You then negotiate the work, deliverables, and inevitably are asked to lower your costs from the already discounted price you initially submitted. The negotiations may go on for months, sometimes more than half a year.

Then you win the contract. Yay! It's time to celebrate. But then nothing happens. After weeks and weeks of follow-up, you are told that the actual project has stalled and will not start for another few months. Thus, you must continue paying for the staff that you have been keeping available since the proposal submission, since they are necessary to deliver the promised work. Oh, and don't forget the interest on the bank loan you took to fund your employees until you are able to finally send an invoice. Plus, the government department you are working for may not pay on time, postponing the reward even further. The longest I've waited was 11 months—what a delayed gratification!

Don't let me scare you; there are many benefits to doing business with the government, but it is not for everyone. You have to be willing to risk the long overdue, but high-value, gratification.

The way you attract customers and partners must also be attractive to you. The reward goes both ways. If doing business with a customer is not rewarding you, then you will most likely discover that you are not meeting the financial success targets you have set for yourself and your business.

Customer Intelligence

The first step in Customer Intelligence is to develop a clear image—for yourself and your organization—as to who your customers are. The first question to ask yourself is "Who is your ideal customer?" To make it easier to put together a composite visual image of just whom you are selling to, here is a group of questions that will help you come up with that answer:

- How old are they?
- What are their hobbies?
- What sports interest them?
- What's their favorite TV show/movie?
- What industries are they in?
- What departments do they fall under?
- What are their job functions and responsibilities?
- Are they members of trade associations? Which ones?
- What is their education level?
- Who are they partnered with professionally?
- What trade or industry magazines do they read?
- What general interest magazines, blogs, and web sites do they read?
- What are their favorite products?

- What types of services do they believe in?

- Whom do they follow or admire on social networks like Twitter, LinkedIn, and Facebook?

- What charities do they support?

It is important to go through this exercise. Before developing these questions, I believed the whole process was rather tedious and a waste of my time. Contrary to my initial thought, I find that it helps me tune in, focus, and bring clarity about who I am serving and how to market to them.

Janet Wood, Executive Vice President of Talent and Leadership at SAP, created a version of her ideal customer and found it extremely valuable. She did this through a workshop offered by Design Thinking, from the Design School at Stanford University. She says, "The one that I was in, a two-day workshop, really focused on attracting and developing talent in SAP. It really changed the game and what we've been trying to do.... Our customers were really our employees and potential employees. You create personas.... You literally go to the point of saying, 'Okay, this persona, her name is Susan, she lives in San Francisco and she just graduated with a BS degree in computer science. She's got a boyfriend. She's working as a waitress during the summer, and she is trying to decide on x.' You go on to create this whole ideal construct."[6]

Wood's goal was to figure out how SAP could be the most attractive to their ideal candidates—the best new graduates in the job market. The trick was, just as it is in Customer Intelligence, to put herself in the mindset of her ideal customer.

"If Susan's working for the summer as a waitress because she's not sure what she wants to do, what would appeal to Susan? She wants to change the world. She's very involved in volunteering, and so on. It's really interesting. At the end you're always thinking back to what does this mean? How does this look to Susan? It sounds pretty straightforward, but it's very, very powerful."

SAP found this exercise so useful that they began to do it with their customers, to help them figure out how to maximize their opportunities with the people they are either currently selling to or the people they want to sell to. "It really gets them thinking about their products and their services and the customer experience in a way that they may not have before, because all of us, even our customers, can get very internally focused," she says.

---

[6] Janet Wood, personal communication, recorded telephone interview with the author, December 18, 2013.

Start a Customer Intelligence Group

Of course, this exercise won't work if you're the only one who knows the answers to these questions. So set up a meeting and perform this exercise as a team. First, invite executives and senior managers from different departments to create their own personal answers to these questions. It's a safe bet they each have a different image of what your ideal customers look and act like.

After everyone shares their responses, work as a group to create a customer composite that works for everybody.

Once everyone is on the same page, continue the process by getting everyone to answer additional questions.

Attracting Your Ideal Customers

The second question, once your group has dreamed up your ideal customer, is this: How can we attract this customer?

For this question, start immediately by brainstorming as a team, rather than individually. One idea will lead to another. Here are a few areas to talk about to get you started:

- Branding
- Advertising
- Public Relations
- Search Engine Optimization (SEO)
- Partnerships
- Word of Mouth

Developing Trust

Once you know how you want to attract your ideal customers, ask your team this third question: How can we earn our customers' trust?

One of the best ways to do this is to use "social proof." Social proof is obtained simply by referencing other people who recommend your products and services.

You may not realize it, but you most likely have a treasure trove of individuals who can serve as your brand champions. Look at your client list. Do any names jump out as those that could be used as references?

Or better yet, implement a process at the end of each client engagement that helps build your testimonial archive. After a pleasant transaction, ask your satisfied customers to write a brief testimonial or recommendation about their experience with your company. The key is to request this while the memory of your excellent product or service is fresh in the customer's mind. Ask if it is possible to post the testimonial on your web site or marketing materials.

The best testimonials discuss why your clients decided to buy from you or hire you and then highlight the ways you helped them solve their problems and address their issues. When prospective customers read the references or testimonials, the content is trusted more because it's coming from a third party.

Where Are Your Ideal Customers?

Here's the fourth question to ask your team: Where do our ideal customers spend their time? Put together a very specific list and consider the following:

- Trade shows
- Partner related events
- Social media
- Forums/blogs
- Associations
- Media
- Directories/databases

How Will You Reach Your Ideal Customers?

The fifth question for your Customer Intelligence team is this: How can we reach our ideal customers? There are many methods you can try, including the following:

- Sponsorships
- Mailers
- Forums/blogs
- Broadcast media (TV, radio, or paper)
- Billboards
- Short Message Systems (SMS)
- Internet marketing and/or digital marketing

- Social media (YouTube, Facebook, Twitter, LinkedIn, Google+, Pinterest, or Tumblr)

- Banner ads

- Content and e-mail marketing

- SEO

- Mobile

You don't need a presence on every platform. Your answers need to be unique to your organization. For example, a government client might not fit in any of the bullets listed above. Professional products and services work best on LinkedIn or SlideShare. Make sure to plan well and keep your customers in mind.

Take every opportunity to be helpful to your potential customers. Many of the media listed above give you the chance to offer information, tips, and tricks that will help your audience accomplish a goal. Don't be afraid to give away free information. That's one great way to build trust.

If there is a forum where someone has an issue or question that you have the answer to, respond. If a journalist opens up a comment thread based on an article and someone has a question, respond. This is also true with fan pages and other social media sites. But, beware. If you are constantly promoting yourself and your company, you will immediately lose respect. Our society continues to slowly evolve from its previous attitude of "sell, sell, sell" to that of "share, share, share."

Figure 3-1 demonstrates how you, your company, and your partners can obtain a clear image of how to reach your ideal customer by answering these five questions above.

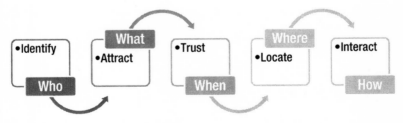

Figure 3-1. Process flow to ideal customer

Habits

Most of the customers you attract to your business will want to retain your products or services. But once you've brought them in, how do you keep them coming back for more?

The secret is to engage your customers and provide a positive, instant gratifying experience (emotional reward). This will create a habit and get your customers to return again and again. Three avenues through which your business can cultivate a relationship with customers are your web site, tablet applications (apps), and mobile apps.

There are some basic design considerations to keep in mind at your touch points with your customer base. Company sites and apps should demonstrate these features:

- Simplicity: They must allow customers to get to data quickly. They must be easy to filter and sort, requiring as few clicks, taps, and other motions as possible.

- Flexibility: They should be easy to use across multiple devices, including mobiles, tablets, laptops, and desktops.

- Bi-directionality: Not only should you be able to communicate with consumers from your sites, but they should be able to communicate with you too. Depending on your product and the size of your customer base, customer service representatives should be accessible via phone, instant chat, e-mail, text, and forums.

- Functionality: Your web sites should load quickly and online business transactions should be easy to complete.

- Security: Data should be secure from security breaches and threats when within web sites and apps as well as when moving from app to app. Customers should be informed that their data is secure.

As you design your web sites and apps, get inside the minds of your customers. Walk in their shoes when you're creating interfaces. Just like a good actor playing a role, think about what motivates your customers and what they want to accomplish thanks to your product.

Another way to form a habit for your customers is to build a community around them. Businesses like Weight Watchers, Facebook, Rosetta Stone, Avon, and Virgin have done this successfully, giving their customers, users, and followers a sense of belonging. This belonging can come from being part of something that is making a big positive impact in society, like fighting obesity or creating more awareness around breast cancer. Or it could come from the ability to connect emotionally with friends and like-minded people from all over the world by sharing similar opinions about your business.

Humans are social beings. We have a strong desire to join with others in places like sports clubs, gyms, teams, and communities. Here are some of the benefits we get by being part of a community:

- Sharing (stories, gossip, ideas)
- Entertainment
- Respect and appreciation
- Being with like-minded people
- Connecting through friendship, compassion, and caring, as well as giving love

Some businesses have been able to create a dynamic environment for their customers and partners. They share information, collaborate on ideas, modify their products through feedback, and spur growth for their customers, partners, and themselves through the use of this collective intelligence.[7] Through community, they invite trust and openness. Figure 3-2 shows the stages that customers go through when forming habits. Observe how these stages can be met through the creation of a dynamic customer community.

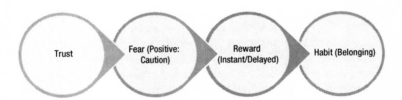

Figure 3-2. Stages to habit

At their core, it's the emotional connection and personal relationship between a business and its customer that makes the business successful. These emotional connections increase interactions and make participation a habit.

Also, emotional social influence can strongly dictate what we try and eventually buy because social networking and online communities foster a strong sense of trust. It's likely that you have either listened to music online or read an article because someone in your social network recommended it.[8]

---

[7]Daria J. Kuss and Mark D. Griffiths, (2011) "Online Social Networking and Addiction—A Review of the Psychological Literature." *Int J Environ Res Public Health* 8(9):3528–3552, www.ncbi.nlm.nih.gov/pmc/articles/PMC3194102/.
[8]Coco Krumme, Manuel Cebrian, Galen Pickard, Sandy Pentland (2012) "Quantifying Social Influence in an Online Cultural Market," PLoS ONE 7(5):e33785, doi:10.1371/journal.pone.0033785.

Business decision makers must engage customers and partners authentically. It is not about getting attention at any cost. It is about creating a relationship—a bond.

Customer Analytics

With the advent of smart mobile devices, we receive coupons, certificates, and updates through apps, e-mail, and text messages—instantly.

You can take customer analytics a lot further today than you could before the mass adoption of the smartphone. For example, in-store behavior intelligence companies have expanded their technology offerings to track a consumer's experience as they shop—by using their mobile device.[9] To ethically incentivize consumers to share personal data with retailers (which they might otherwise prefer to keep private), stores are now offering instant rewards like coupons. If you are within a certain radius of the store, a GPS tracking mechanism will locate you and then send you a special deal customized to your previous purchase data. It's getting to the point where the salesperson will be able to greet you by name upon your arrival with three sweaters in your favorite colors—and in your size—that are discounted just for you because of your decision to come into the store.

Once you enter a shop, barcode or QR code scanning capabilities offer retailers more opportunities to engage with you. When you pay for your items, the check-out clerk may ask for your e-mail as a method to send receipts. Then, voila, there is a coupon in your inbox for your next shopping trip that may be personalized the same way Amazon makes recommendations for other books—by looking at what you bought and comparing it with items purchased by other customers who bought the same thing.

Tracking technology can also be used to identify ways to improve store products, promotions, and the overall customer experience. You probably don't even recognize the cameras and facial recognition software that track your expressions and predict your next move while shopping.

Many retail businesses use Customer Intelligence to continually evolve and improve their business. We can all learn from savvy retailers when thinking about how to understand and engage our customer. Your customer analytics should focus on the behavior and mindset of your customers as well as that

---

[9]Stephanie Clifford and Quentin Hardy, "Attention, Shoppers: Store Is Tracking Your Cell." *The New York Times*, p. A1, July 14, 2013, www.nytimes.com/2013/07/15/business/attention-shopper-stores-are-tracking-your-cell.html.

of others who are engaged with your videos, web sites, blogs, etc. Here are three questions you should ask:

- Why are your customers doing business with you?
- Why are they receptive to your message, brand, products, and services?
- How are the audiences who read and watch the material you put out engaging with that material? (your media customers, whose level of interest indicates they may be "pre-customers")

Understanding your existing customers and what motivates them (as well as your pre-customers for your videos and social media campaigns) is the key to keeping them as loyal members of your company's family. When you know what they want, you can give them more.

Data for customer analytics can come from various sources, such as the following:

- Social media
- Web clickstreams
- Sales reports
- Call detail records
- Customer service
- Service and delivery records
- Contract management
- Order management

The data that is derived from customer analytics can help transform and add value to your relationship with customers, and even your partners. Pay attention to some of your customers' behavior. What is the retention rate? What are they marking on their surveys? How do they prefer to communicate with your company?

Companies should have a list of data sources they continually monitor and track to understand customer engagement, such as the following:

- Customer experience
- Satisfaction surveys
- Social media engagement: click-through to webinars, videos, and podcasts
- Communication preference: e-mail, text, chat, or phone

- Customer transaction types
- Online purchases
- Service history
- Retention rate
- Education and/or training
- Downloading of white papers, data sheets, and case studies
- Forums and blog comments

You might think that some of the bullets overlap, but they are indeed separate. For example, customer experience is a different entity than satisfaction surveys. Customer experience is a written or verbal description by your customers detailing what they gained or lost by doing business with you. If they've had a good experience, you can ask them for permission to use a portion of the material they've communicated as a testimonial. Satisfaction surveys are usually multiple-choice affairs, with a few fill-in-the-blank questions drawing out either a positive experience with your company or areas you need to improve.

Another item worth examining is the actual cost per deliverable versus the perceived satisfaction of that deliverable. Did your customers think the cost was too high, against the value they received, or did they believe the value they received was more than expected?

Behavior and Predictive Analytics

The two primary areas that drive customer analytics are behavior and prediction. Amazon has mastered these, connecting your search and purchase behavior, then predicting what else you might like by comparing it to other customers who have viewed the same things.

There's one thing you should keep in mind. If the criteria for your ideal customer has changed from your current customers, even slightly, the past behaviors of your current customers are no longer the only valid indicators of future predictive analytics. Let's say you sell a product that tracks body activity movements. You had previously identified your ideal customer segment as runners, and subsequently marketed to them. At a recent meeting, however, your team determined that your customer segment has expanded from runners to include the health conscious. So you now might need to think about how to market to customers who drink tea, golf, or dance. Since those people aren't in your customer database, analyzing your current customers won't help you understand this new, untapped group.

Digital Analytics

If you're staying with the same ideal customer, though, there is a lot of data out there to be collected, including information from your web site, social media, mobile apps, CRM application, sales system, customer support, and more.

Digital analytics enables you to determine the strategy direction your company needs to take. There are dozens of tools to choose from to help you manage this process. But first you need to understand what is best for your type of business. The point of these analytics is to determine if marketing activities and engagements are heading in the right direction, and what, if anything, needs to change.

Figure 3-3 shows some of the main sources of customer digital interaction with your brand.

Figure 3-3. Examples of digital analytics touch points

Digital analytics is a continually evolving process that benefits all parties, since the feedback collected will then be channeled into improving the product and benefiting society on the whole. As the public demands additional capabilities such as better speed, performance, flexibility, and more, you have to continually improve your business by exploring new possibilities. The good news is that many IT vendors can scale to your needs, thanks to cloud-based solutions. Make a plan first and then look for a solution that you can grow into. Rethink what it is you want, based on your current state and where you want to go.

Another key area to analyze is the type of digital media messaging you are utilizing. Is it paid, owned, or earned?

- Paid: Variable messaging costs such as PR, branding, advertisements, paid search engine marketing, and banners

- Owned: Your own in-house content, such as web sites, blogs, and social media accounts and pages

- Earned: Media exposure from articles written about you, conversations held by your advocates and influencers, and word of mouth

Companies frequently use a mix of paid, owned, and earned media, as shown in Figure 3-4. Understanding your outbound marketing methods enables you to better track and monitor your return on investment (ROI) as it relates to digital analytics.

Figure 3-4. Mixed media types of digital analytics

Everything you're tracking should measure your progress toward a goal. Are you trying to solve a problem? Do you want to see if a certain campaign is driving attention? Are you tracking feedback about a new launch?

Within digital analytics, I will highlight two basic data sources: web analytics and mobile analytics.

Web Analytics

Did you ever go to a travel website looking for flights or hotels, then switch to another site to compare deals? When you click on the alternative site, all of your search criteria has been magically filled out on the new site's forms—the number of days traveling, where you're departing from, and where your destination is. How does that happen? Your information is being tracked through the use of cookies and other devices.

This information helps companies make decisions about how to handle everything from marketing campaigns to the exact words and pictures they use on their web sites. Web analytics helps collect what happens before a customer buys, how long customers stay on a web site, and even when in the process they jump off—for example, when they abandon their shopping cart instead of buying. Mastering this analysis and responding correctly to the information you receive can lead to revenue growth and repeatedly attracting and retaining customers. The correct use of web analytics helps determine if you're receiving the proper return on your company's marketing investments.

Web analytics also helps businesses evaluate what type of online marketing is most beneficial. For example, if you are looking for a proactive outbound marketing activity and need to know what to choose, web analytics can inform you as to the most appropriate options.

In the recent past, web analytics would only measure simple information like the number of visitors to your site, search engine keywords leading to your site, and how long a customer stayed on your site. This is known as web clickstream analysis. These days, web analytics has become more sophisticated, as businesses are demanding to know more and more about their customers.

Understanding Your Audience

The Department of Veterans Affairs (VA) uses YouTube to get its message out in video format. The VA has generated over 500 videos, each with an average length of three minutes. It even has its own YouTube Channel, with an introductory promotional video.

YouTube has become one of the top search engines in the world. More and more people are getting their information via video, and YouTube provides businesses with plenty of useful analytics to help them optimize the ability to attract viewers and keep them engaged.

The VA is one of many organizations utilizing video and other social media formats to improve their ROI. Analytics allow you to learn your audience demographics, how long they watch each video, and understand which videos attract the most viewers.

The goals of your videos should be to build trust in a way that either educates, entertains, or benefits your customers, without seeming a blatant commercial. No one is searching YouTube in order to be sold something. If people do search for commercials, it's for entertainment purposes or curiosity, or maybe they're nostalgically looking for old Pepsodent commercials.

Mobile Analytics

Mobile analytics looks at how your customers use your company's apps. The design and functionality for mobile apps need to be appealing and usable for customers.

Though analytics for mobile apps can tell you the number and demographics of new and active users, the most important index that businesses can track is how their customers interact with an app. Are the apps converting customers to become retained, satisfied followers or advocates? Are customers in the habit of using the business's mobile app? As we discussed earlier in the chapter, customers want to form habits with apps that provide them with rewards of some kind.

Detailed analytical reports about customer behavior with mobile apps typically answer the following sorts of questions:

- How do screens rank in popularity?

- How often do customers use the app?

- How much time is the app used for?

- Is a promotional code or coupon being used?

- What keywords are being used as a customer searches for the app?

Like all analytics, mobile analytics should be used as a method for process improvement. What tactics connect with customers and keep them engaged and coming back for more? What bores them? What drives customers to make certain decisions? Good mobile app intelligence tries to understand the customers' unconscious habits. The trick to attracting customers is to learn from your analytics what makes the ultimate positive experience for them, then modify your processes and systems, and realign the strategies and tactics involved.

Consensus

Customer Intelligence is about mapping and wiring your business mind for customer success. Not your success or your company's success— your customers' success. Look at your organization. Do you have customer data sources separated by department? Do you have a central way of capturing customer analytics? How is the overall performance of customer relationship evaluated?

In the next chapter on Data Intelligence, I highlight the significance of consolidation, sharing, and collaboration for visual communication and decisions across the business for everything you do.

Data
Intelligence

Reinvent and Recreate Your Business

The eye sees only what the mind is prepared to comprehend.

— Robertson Davies, *Tempest-Tost*

How do you bring together teams from different business lines to develop a more cohesive approach to connect and converse about critical decisions?

That is the crux of your task when you utilize *Data Transformational Intelligence.*

Data Intelligence is about the process and steps to synchronously communicate and interpret data across teams and groups of individuals within a department, across departments, with third party vendors, partners, and even sometimes between two or more organizations.

The Power of Visual Data

Visual data can be a powerful ally when you want to make sure the information you are communicating is understood and received in the way that you intend. You see, people within a department may be familiar with their own data, but when seven departments or organizations each bring their own data to the table, there's too much to read and absorb. You need some kind of shorthand that enables you to quickly get to the heart of what the data means and that lets you communicate transparently about the information it represents. Visual data lets you accomplish those tasks.

I once was tasked with providing a visual performance management strategy plan to the United States Postal Service (USPS) CIO office that would allow for collaboration, communication, and sharing of data across the enterprise's different departments. I discovered that decision makers crave instant, accurate, and reliable visuals of their data. Sharing information in a visual format makes it easier for executives and senior managers in different departments to connect about critical decisions that affect them all.

How the Brain Perceives Visual Information

Let's take a minute to explore how your brain processes visual information. When you see something—be it text, a static image, or a moving object— light stimulates the retina, giving you a visual perception that is controlled by the visual cortex. The visual cortex is located within the occipital lobe of your brain, as shown previously in Figure 1-1. This process happens very fast. The visual cortex is made up of specialized neurons that turn the sensations received from the optic nerve into meaningful images. Perception is how the brain interprets the environment based on information that the sensory organs, including the eyes, pick up.

However, the process of interpreting what you saw does not stop there. The visual perception of what you saw and—note here—paid attention to then sends signals to the cerebral cortex of your brain. I emphasize "paid attention to" because the brain has blind spots or gaps where you don't notice things, causing you to fill in your own interpretation of events. The visual cortex simply fills in the small hole in your vision with similar patterns from the surrounding areas, so you never notice what's missing.

The cerebral cortex of your brain is also where the cognitive conscious part of what you saw kicks in. This reaction is similar to turning on a light switch. The cerebral cortex interprets what you visually *paid attention to* and then stores that interpretation in your memory.

Thanks to this process, orienting data in a visual format will help ensure that your audience focuses on the information you want them to pay attention to.

Creating Impact with Visual Designs

Since visual data can be so effective, let's talk about how to optimize your visual designs so that they have the highest impact possible.

Why are some gaming applications more successful than others? Part of what makes these games so addictive is the pure simplicity of their design. If you've ever been hooked on a game like Bejeweled Blitz or Candy Crush Saga, and played it for an extended period of time—say 45 minutes straight—you may have experienced the phenomenon of closing your eyes and involuntarily seeing the jewels or candies from the game.

That couldn't happen with a more complex design.

So if we want to design an easy to perceive message, both the overall image and the items within it need to be in simple, bite-sized chunks. Since an overload of data causes most people to feel overwhelmed, you only want to display data that is critical to helping everyone make effective and well-informed decisions.

For example, if you were assessing customer support issues, here are a few icons you might consider for use in your visual report in Figure 4-1:

- Case Management System icon > displayed as a briefcase showing the number of cases that are particularly important

- Help Desk icon > image of a help desk support person representing the number of support tickets logged

- Phone icon > demonstrated to represent volume of calls

Figure 4-1. Visual cues individually displayed

As we have learned, visual representations of data need to have common definitions and interpretations within the organization. For example, if your case management system is down, causing a high volume of incidents and longer calls, using visual cues to convey the message takes less time than using long and descriptive text. When your company knows what these images signify, communicating with a single image icon gets the message across more expeditiously, as shown in Figure 4-2.

Figure 4-2. Visual cues collectively displayed

Data Confusion

Visual data, in particular, and any form of data can unfortunately also be used to create data confusion. Data confusion occurs when numbers are skewed to prove a point, gain votes, or start an argument. Something unproven, or even untrue, can now seem like the truth. Data confusion is most powerful when it's visual in nature, but can still occur when it's not. You'd be surprised at how often politicians, members of the media, researchers, executives, and even authors use misleading data. In meetings, I have seen marketing statistics showcasing 100% customer satisfaction. Wow, that seems pretty impressive, but what does such a claim mean? How many customers is that based on? In reality, it could be from a sample size of one. While this information is valid, it doesn't paint the proper picture and unaware individuals may make decisions based on faulty "facts." You wouldn't want to base your decision to move forward with a program if only one client had reported 100% satisfaction. You'd want more data and feedback to ensure that the program will be successful when it's launched.

While many companies intentionally use data confusion as a marketing weapon, it occurs unintentionally with even greater frequency. Often data is presented in a visual reporting type format—charts, graphs, or icons—that creates inaccurate impressions. Other times you are given numerous amounts of data in report formats that you have no idea what to do with. You don't know how to interpret the data, what you're looking for, or what is missing. You are so overwhelmed by the sheer quantity of information that you depend on others to translate the data for you in order to make a decision. But, there's a catch.

This approach allows for errors and misinterpretation, and this is not something you can afford to have happen. Each individual is trained to visually encode and interpret information—shapes, color, text, and images—in a certain way. The brain is primed to focus attention on what it has previously stored. Therefore, when there are multiple people involved, individuals have different perceptions based on what they visually recall from their past experience. This is why disagreements and conflicts can occur. You cannot assume everyone involved will interpret data the same way.

Further, everyone involved may not have the same definition of the data being presented. For example, if you ask three different senior managers for the average units sold last year, the responses could vary widely since there are at least three different definitions of an "average" when it comes to statistics.

- Senior Manager A calculates the average based on the *mean*—the total sum of all numbers divided by the quantity of numbers

- Senior Manager B calculates the average based on the *median*—the middle value of the list of numbers spread in numerical order

- Senior Manager C calculates the average based on the *mode*—the value that occurs most often

Table 4-1 shows the number of units sold per month in a given year.

Table 4-1. Number of units sold per month

	Jan	Feb	Mar	Apr	May	Jun	Jul	Aug	Sep	Oct	Nov	Dec
Units Sold	23	33	42	31	23	32	23	37	48	33	48	47

- Senior Manager A's "average" is 35.
  - (23 + 33 + 42 + 31 + 23+ 32 + 23 + 37 + 48 + 33 + 48 + 47) / 12 months = 35

- Senior Manager B's "average" is 33. B hears the word average but calculates the median.
  - (23, 23, 23, 31, 32, 33, 33, 37, 42, 47, 48, 48) = numbers rewritten in order. Since there are 12 months, the middle would be the 6th number. The median is 33.

- Senior Manager C's "average" is 23 since the number of units sold most often is 23.

The resulting numbers can vary considerably, as can their significance. This issue mostly occurs in a siloed organization, where there is no communication of universal definitions between departments, as opposed to an integrated one. Even in an integrated environment, definitions and processes need to be continually checked and improved, due to constantly changing influences and pressures that occur in an organization. For example, external mandates, big data, and social connections can change the statistics you utilize.

One of the questions you need to consistently ask yourself is "Why should I believe the information I have before me is accurate?" How can you make sure that you're not being unduly influenced by data confusion when making decisions? How do you gain visual clarity, create a common language, and make sure everyone is seeing and interpreting information in the same way across the enterprise?

A few years back, my team and I presented to 12 decision makers and influencers at the Small Business Administration (SBA) about a type of performance reporting for the CIO's office. At the time, the SBA's CIO had a preference to see data visually laid out in bubble charts. "Why specifically bubbles?" I asked. Her answer was that it just made sense to her. She knew how to interpret the information when it was presented in that format. It was in her comfort zone, and she had a positive visual emotional experience with it. But, the resulting issue was making sure that visual format was easily understood by those who reported to her and by those who were collecting the data.

Unified Data Clarity

So how do you get everyone on the same page when interpreting and communicating information about the same data—text, numbers, images, shapes, and symbols? You need to have conversations about what data means to the organization. The standards that you establish need to be learned, shared, and encoded through training and repetition. Repetition as a group will help to establish habits so that everyone jointly recalls, interprets, and translates the information in a unified way. This newly learned behavior will minimize risk and increase consistency and confidence in the information when presented both internally and externally.

Data Intelligence

Do you have a Data Intelligence of your organization, department, or division? Data Intelligence is built on the Nine C's—collaborating, consolidating, communicating, collecting, connecting, coordinating, changing, conversing, and converting, as shown in Figure 4-3.

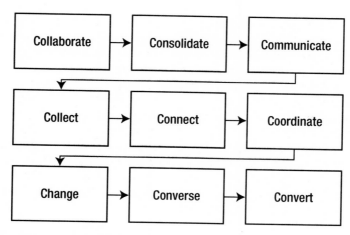

Figure 4-3. Nine C's of Data Intelligence

As we discussed earlier, Data Intelligence represents the need to universally interpret data by teams and groups of individuals within a department, across departments, with third party vendors, partners, and even sometimes between two or more organizations, as is the case with the Defense Technical Information Center (DTIC).

One of DTIC's main functions is to serve as the research and engineering hub for the Department of Defense (DoD), providing and sharing scientific and technical information to and with other agencies. DTIC is also a web hosting provider for DoD agencies. Because of these critical roles, DTIC needs answers to certain questions from the agencies and partners it supports:

- Why does this agency need this data?
- Who in the agency need access to this data?
- What types of data do they need?
- When do they need this data?
- Where do changes need to be made to access the data?
- How is this data provided?

When my company worked with DTIC, we helped them outline their security infrastructure and established a plan for data security considerations as data was stored and passed between agencies. We also helped them understand who had access to the data, at which security levels, and plotted the data flow to be seamless between agencies. Here, the client's resulting initiative was to have an integrated and collaborative security plan to share data across agencies.

Integration of data across different organizations occurs frequently and is very common in mergers and acquisitions. Typically, though, organizations are looking for visual insight and intelligence into their own company as they migrate from a siloed to an integrated environment. When I worked with the Pension Benefit Guaranty Corporation (PBGC), a federal government agency that protects pensions, I led a team to support the integration of information, processes, and technologies of two major departments within the agency—the Office of Chief Counsel (OCC) and the Department of Insurance Supervision and Compliance (DISC). The two departments were separate and needed to be integrated. I helped them to integrate their legal matter management system and the financial case management system into one customized system that provided data intelligence for executives and decision makers, so they could better support their customers.

The Six Reporter Questions and the Nine C's

Planning for Data Intelligence starts by applying the Nine C's no matter how large or complex you think your business goals, objectives, and initiatives are. The Nine C's provide insight into what is happening with the data. All of the Nine C's need to be considered in order to maximize Data Intelligence. You also need to answer the six reporter questions all journalists are taught to include in their stories—why, who, what, when, where, and how as shown in Figure 4-4.

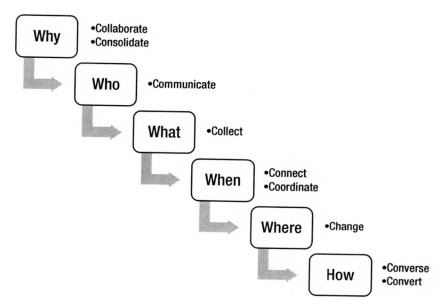

Figure 4-4. Six reporter questions and the Nine C's

Here's how you map the six reporter questions to the Nine C's to gain Data Intelligence:

- **Why** - Why is there a need to **Collaborate** and/or **Consolidate** the data?

- **Who** - Who needs to **Communicate** with the data?

- **What** - What data do I need to **Collect**?

- **When** - When do I need to **Connect** and **Coordinate** efforts about the data?

- **Where** - Where do I need to make **Changes** about the data?

- **How** - How do I **Converse** about the data and **Convert** to new ways of interacting with it?

Using PBGC's data plan as an example, Table 4-2 demonstrates the call to action by using the six reporter questions with the Nine C's.

Table 4-2. Data Intelligence and the Six Reporter Questions

Six Reporter Questions	Data Plan Call to Action Using PBGC as an Example
Why is there a need to collaborate and/or consolidate the data?	To integrate two departments (OCC & DISC)
Who needs to communicate with the data?	Attorneys, paralegals, financial analysts, actuaries
What data do I need to collect?	Financial data about pensions
When do I need to connect and coordinate efforts about the data?	Transferring financial data to legal matter
Where do I need to make changes about the data?	Pension plan status changes to "termination"
How do I converse about the data and convert to new ways of interacting with it?	Automate processes and approval notifications

Let's dive a bit deeper into the Data Intelligence when the six reporter questions are mapped to the Nine C's.

Why Collaborate and Consolidate

What kind of new initiative are you bringing to your company? Whether it's big data, business intelligence, mobility, cloud, governance, compliance, or security, you must start off knowing why you need to collaborate and consolidate,

For example, DTIC planned to create the DTIC Information Cloud for the purpose of building a knowledge-sharing community where DoD researchers and acquisition professionals could find people, ask questions, and search databases of different topics. The question of "Why is there a need to collaborate on the data?" was answered for DTIC in a clear and resounding way and set the tone for the project.

That clarity is crucial to obtain for whatever initiative you are bringing to the table.

Collaborating

The word "collaboration" may have multiple definitions across your company. My definition is as follows: *Collaboration happens when teams of people join together in order to plan and execute activities with the purpose of transforming and driving value through improvement of performance.*

Performance improvement can be accomplished across multiple organizations, departments, divisions, or teams.

You are welcome to use my definition or refine it for your organization. Just make sure everyone else has the same definition.

Consolidating

The act of consolidating is usually interpreted to mean the merger or acquisition of companies. However, internal consolidation within an organization happens quite frequently. When you do decide to consolidate ideas and processes, there needs to be mental preparation and readiness. Transitioning from a siloed organization to an integrated one requires managing the flow of information, processes, and technologies across the company.

It's important to have an intelligence hub from which governance, risk, and compliance can be managed. This will be the central repository of unified definitions, processes, and enterprise-wide data oversight. The mission of the intelligence hub is to make sure the company's vision, strategies, plans, and processes work and function in harmony.

Who Communicates

Who needs to communicate with the data?

In the PBGC example, attorneys, paralegals, financial analysts, and actuaries are listed as the key individuals interacting with the data. But, it is crucial to identify others who could be impacted by updates, changes, or modifications done to the data. Also, who else might benefit from improved data, thanks to collaboration and/or consolidation? Who else needs insight into Data Intelligence?

Many do not account for external parties that also need Data Intelligence, such as partners, clients, vendors, and auditors. Have you accounted for others within your company who might not require daily Data Intelligence, but would still benefit from occasional insight into the data? Examples could be board members, compliance officers, audit officers, the legal team, risk officers, or executives. Think about who else is potentially impacted by the *why* of your efforts. Particularly when you are setting targets.

Let me give you an example of a scenario encountered by a client because they didn't include their vendors when setting targets, and thus didn't factor in a significant vendor data point. There was also a problem with the client's documentation that further complicated things.

My international client's IT department was seeing a sharp increase in volume of dissatisfaction calls, support tickets, and poor ratings from their own internal customers, the business users. What was going on? It turned out that the telecommunications was down and IT was expected to respond within four hours. Four hours had gone by and there was no response from IT, let alone a resolution. IT was waiting on Verizon to respond to them. They had a formal service level agreement (SLA) with their third party provider, Verizon, and Verizon's response time to the IT department was eight hours, a very large variance from IT's promise of four hours.

Unlike with Verizon, IT did not have a formal internal SLA with its business users. Although it was ideal for IT to respond to internal business users within a set time frame, they were not accountable for it—and reasonably so. If there had been formal internal documentation and agreement of expectation, then the gap between the third party and IT's time frame would have been detected.

Don't Forget About Your Customers

You might think that your customers are not part of your collaborative data efforts. This is not true. You most likely already collaborate with them through forums, surveys, and other means of communication. How about feedback received through your support call center? Think about the various ways you are capturing information from your customers for improvement.

What to Collect

Do you have a clear idea of what data you need to collect?

To help you picture this, gather and document requirements. Assess the impacts, both internally and externally. Areas affected by the data could be finances, customer satisfaction, or safety. For example, let's say you have a project initiative called "Bring-Your-Own-Device" (BYOD), where all employees need to provide their own tablet or smartphone to be used at least partially for work purposes. Your *why* is that everyone must be able to interact with the new applications your business is using, understand the data flow, and then use that information to improve business performance. Your *who* refers to decision makers from HR, legal, financial procurement, IT, and employees. You start collecting the *what* by asking questions. Here are some sample questions you might consider:

- Who buys the device and pays for its data plan?

- Who will have access to what data?

- Should all charges be reimbursed or should there be a set fixed amount covered?

- What are the security requirements at the different levels (devices, applications, and data)?

- What type of support will be provided (device or corporate application running on the device)?

- What devices will be supported?

- Is this program in compliance with other corporate initiatives (such as Green IT)?

When you explore *why* this new initiative was created, you can begin to better understand how it can be used to collaborate and communicate data with employees, partners, and clients.

Visual Analytics

The process of analyzing and deciding what data you need to capture for Data Intelligence can be enhanced by visual analytics, which can help determine what data needs to be collected and displayed visually as well as how to organize it into measures, metrics, and key performance indicators (KPIs). The target for the *why* needs to also be defined.

When you tell someone a story, it paints a picture. For example, I was looking to travel from Washington, DC to New York during the holidays. Looking at the number of flights, I could see they were scheduled to depart on the hour every hour. However, some flights were either being cancelled or delayed due to snow on the East Coast.

The measures, metrics, and KPIs, as bulleted below, help bring the visual to life, so a key decision maker clearly sees what action must be taken. As mentioned before, when communicating this information, it helps to use simple, easy-to-understand graphics, like the briefcase icons shown in the customer support example.

- Measures = number of flights
- Metrics = number of flights per day x every hour
- KPIs = weather conditions

In this scenario, the decision maker is the customer for the airlines and airport—me. However, there are other people who will find this data valuable, who need to be made aware of it. Can you create a list of the *who*? Who else besides the customer would need to have visibility into weather conditions and status of flights?

Manufacturers delivering products via air travel and also the airlines themselves need to be kept abreast of flight status, as they are linked with revenue and other key impacts. These organizations could lose revenue and get off track from their target based on the goal that has been linked with the KPI (the weather condition). The target is measured against a baseline such as last year's flight results within a set time frame, say the holiday season. The visual data could reflect a range of performance indicators that lets the viewer see flight statuses.

As part of your requirement gathering, how do you determine when it is best to connect the data to other resources? For example, when is the best time to have the customer connect with the data regarding delayed or canceled flights?

Operational Analytics

Now it is time to connect the dots and review the coordination of the data flow itself. Operational analytics bridges the gap and connects people, processes, technology, and information. For operational analytics to be properly monitored and tracked—sometimes in real-time—there needs to be an intelligence hub placed in this area as well. Practices and architecture are also implemented in this phase to ensure compliance issues, government regulations, and audit requirements are met. The team that makes up the intelligence hub will address how the data is to be organized and integrated, in addition to accounting for security and privacy.

The intelligence hub also coordinates which steps must follow each other when communicating data across the organization. When a specific data touch point is completed, then whatever comes next must begin. This can also involve the monitoring of which activities are best practices and industry standards, such as minimizing cost, managing risk, and eliminating security threats. You want to get to the point of being able to visually detect and handle issues that arise from day-to-day operational activities before they occur. To get there, you must continuously improve your processes.

Where to Change

When you have addressed the *why, who, what,* and *when,* you can start to look for other opportunities to improve your organization. You ask, "*Where do I need to make changes?*"

Imagine there is an external regulation that has changed. You need to incorporate it into your business operations and to your data processes. Where do you make those changes? Visually knowing where the data is stored allows you to address those issues more easily. That's also true if the need to make a change comes internally, as is the case with a new initiative. Today it is all about cloud computing, big data, business intelligence, and mobility. Tomorrow it will be about something else. Having a framework in the form of documented approaches and processes allows you to take a proactive approach to changing environments.

How to Converse and Convert

How will you converse about changes that are needed? What if those needs require innovations to your products or your procedures? How do you handle forward thinking in your organization?

Is there a plan in place for who will do what to take proactive measures? A bad scenario is when you need to react to a change and you have no plan, not knowing how the changes will impact different areas of the business.

Create a visual map for how your organization will take action. How can you identify the audience who will be impacted? Do the changes require a corporate communication message? Will the change require training? What methods are in place for handling clients? Is support or customer care prepared to answer and respond to client inquiries? How do you create conversations about the data? Do you capture or disseminate data through social media, web forums, online communities, or virtual events?

As you brainstorm with different people within your organization, you will create a specific, fine-tuned process plan. Observe the way that data travels. Assess the impact, issues, and risks, plus identify the root causes of any issues that arise.

Is there a way to introduce newer, innovative ways to do things? How about converting traditional communication to mobile communication? How would you strategize for a program such as Bring-Your-Own-Device (BYOD)? A BYOD program can increase employee performance, morale, and productivity, plus enable increased collaboration and quicker response time to information, requests, etc. How will you decide which applications are acceptable within the organization, and for whom? How will corporate data be managed on employee devices, while keeping personal information confidential?

As you can probably tell by now, the how questions involve creativity, innovation, and inspiration. The how is not an individual but a collective, mastermind effort. Mastermind Intelligence will be discussed in the next chapter.

Step Back

Technologists, scientists, and analysts are becoming more engaged with understanding organizational behavior on a microlevel and how it applies to the organization as a whole. Look within your organization, stop, and stand back. Who, if anyone, is championing the study and improvement of group dynamics, behavior, interaction, collaboration, and communication?

At the very least, reread the Data Intelligence section detailing the formula. Then, step back and hold the magnifying glass to your own organization. What changes would you make? How would you apply them? How would you promote creativity, innovation, teamwork, and productivity?

Step outside yourself and your organization and then really dare to visualize. What do you see?

Mastermind Intelligence

Rewire Your Business

New ideas are the lifeblood of any dynamic company. Eliciting fresh thoughts and perspectives on company offerings, marketing campaigns, or customer needs ensures that your company stays competitive through the innovation of new products, services, and ways to solve customer problems.

More than likely, the people in your organization have many great ideas to improve every aspect of your business. However, many companies can get so caught up in daily responsibilities that they fail to set aside time to generate new ideas. Leadership can too easily forget that innovation can be unearthed from many corners: sales people, customer liaisons, product designers, and, of course, marketing teams.

One of the best ways to generate top-notch ideas is through Mastermind Intelligence, which takes the basic concepts of brainstorming and makes them part of the culture of your company. The key is to create a nonjudgmental, respectful environment where each individual is committed to being creative and helpful. Support given during brainstorming is about honesty, respect, and compassion. It is not a competition. Rather, it is about everyone sincerely wanting to achieve a common goal and then finding the best ways to make it happen. "If you have people bringing their own ideas to the table, you get more ideas," says Gary Quinn, President and CEO of FalconStor, an international software company. "It just becomes exponential because now their ideas are your ideas. Before you know it, you have fostered an environment of creativity and ideas."[1]

---

[1] Gary Quinn, personal communication by voice-recorded face-to-face interview with author, Long Island, NY, November 19, 2013. Passim throughout this chapter.

Leading with Innovation

The best risk you can take is on a new idea. That very idea could solve a client's problem or provide a new feature or function that your customers did not have access to before.

Lead and be acknowledged for innovation. Strive to establish and maintain a track record of tackling difficult problems in new ways. Create new, disruptive technology that allows you to quickly gain market share.

What type of corporate culture do you want to have? Does your team embrace change and innovation? Create a fountain of new ideas.

Without a pipeline of new ideas, it becomes challenging to grow in a competitive market.

Leveraging Mastermind Practices

Cary Bayer, founder of Bayer Communications, a corporate coaching company that helps executives achieve continuous company breakthroughs, believes that Mastermind Intelligence creates bigger ideas than that of normal thinking. "The Mastermind concept is designed to bring out the kinds of ideas that normally won't surface in an organization," he says, "especially if there is a good facilitator there to guide."[2]

An ongoing Mastermind Intelligence culture can transform your business—not just within your organization, but also with your partners and even your clients.

Mastermind practices can be of two types: (1) small group meetings that elicit a broad range of ideas, and (2) more formal meetings where senior leaders assess the top ideas.

Mastermind Intelligence results in increased originality of thought. When executives are launching new programs or consolidating existing ones, they are often uncomfortable thinking creatively. "They're afraid that they'll be seen as not grounded enough or not conservative enough within the culture of the organization," says Bayer.

The nonjudgmental tone of the ideation phase of Mastermind Intelligence creates an environment where all ideas are welcome and enhance the flow of creativity.

---

[2]Cary Bayer, personal communication by recorded telephone interview with author, January 3, 2014. Passim throughout this chapter.

This environment makes it easier to be inventive and sparks questions such as, *"What can we create here?" "What can we imagine that is out of the ordinary?"* and *"How can we make sure that there is no 'wrong answer,' allowing the best ideas to emerge?"*

According to Quinn, another benefit of a joint Mastermind mentality is employee buy-in: "We just recently got 30 people together to build a product roadmap together. It was no longer my roadmap, it wasn't the investor's roadmap—it is the people's roadmap. Now, they can't say they don't believe in it, because they were part of the creation."

Create an environment conducive to sharing thoughts and ideas by asking people at all levels for feedback, keeping them informed about goals and projects and demonstrating how their past input has positively impacted your product offerings or services.

Implementing Mastermind Intelligence in Weekly Meetings

There are several ways to bring Mastermind Intelligence to your organization.

One way is to designate part of your weekly meeting time as an open session to discuss ideas, challenges, or opportunities. Each attendee can raise different topics. Often companies become so mired in everyday details that they don't take time to really assess opportunities across the organization. As mentioned previously, try something different to break routine, such as changing the meeting time or location, so that people don't become so used to a standing meeting that they become creatively lax.

During the meeting, each attendee should be encouraged to bring up a pressing topic. And then, don't ignore it. I've often seen a senior leader state an opinion followed by no one challenging it. People feel uncomfortable speaking up in meetings, especially to challenge their boss. So if you are the one facilitating the meeting, don't overtly offer your opinion on a topic. Instead, ask a question and ask everyone present to anonymously jot down their opinions on paper.

"The human being is ultimately a creative being but . . . fear-based thinking stifles that," says Bayer. "As one begins to feel less threatened and therefore safe and relaxed, it becomes easier to open up and express opinions. Observe people at parties. At first, some people are tense and quiet, but once they start to relax, it tends to stimulate a more creative way of being."

Focus on having one topic on the table that needs to be addressed. This will allow people to really focus their resources, support, and energy on that one issue. In smaller businesses, a shift in the direction of campaign or in a program could immediately change the business overnight. In large ones, it may be more difficult to determine the overall impact brought on by a new idea.

Get people to write one or two solutions or ideas down on a piece of paper. Then you can truly elicit involvement by providing an environment where it feels safe to express an opinion.

Once people are comfortable sharing, have them vote on the most interesting ideas. Then focus the rest of the meeting on those ideas. Make sure the discussion remains on the idea, not the person who presented it.

Businesswide Mastermind Intelligence Sessions

To fully implement Financial Intelligence, Customer Intelligence, and Data Intelligence, it is useful to have businesswide Mastermind Intelligence sessions. These sessions can be a day - or even a weekend - long affair that takes place offsite. In an ideal world, you might do these as often as quarterly, but your initial goal should be at least annually, with semi-annually being even better. These meetings don't need to include everyone from your company—just representatives from all departments, preferably at all levels, including the people who directly interface with customers. If you've thought about your own organization as you read the previous chapters, there are a lot of possible topics that should come to mind. These are topics that your organization ought to look at holistically, with input from a wide range of departments. Make a list of these topics and use them to guide the agenda for your first businesswide Mastermind Intelligence session.

You can also prompt additional topics ahead of time from the people you're inviting.

Giving each topic an appropriate title will make a difference in the response you get. Neuroscientist Dr. Paul Zak, Director of the multidisciplinary Center for Neuroeconomics Studies (CNS) at Claremont Graduate University, believes that you can get the best results by communicating the emotional benefits of what you're trying to accomplish. "This purpose really has to be kind of what I call a core purpose, or how does your organization improve people's lives," he says. "If that's transmitted clearly and consistently, then it reinforces that we're all on the same team."[3]

---

[3]Paul Zak, personal communication by recorded telephone interview with author, December 30, 2013. Passim throughout this chapter.

Zak says that transactional purposes, such as creating the best product at the best price, are not as motivational. Ideally, "the purpose is not about maximizing sales. It's about improving life and it's easy to motivate teams across the company to be more cooperative."

While you're selecting employees to attend the session, don't just look at departments and levels. Mastermind practices should include the key influencers and decision makers, but they should also include anyone who tends to be good at pulling together disparate ideas and seeing connections, themes, and patterns.

According to Zak, it also makes sense to have people with a variety of backgrounds present. "There's a lot of evidence that work groups diverse in gender, background, and ethnicity are the most innovative. There's pretty good emerging science suggesting that real diversity is important. It's not just the color of your skin or the language you speak, but the way you're trained, where you grew up, and certainly your gender."

Make sure you notify session attendees about topics at least a few weeks in advance. Though a portion of your Mastermind Intelligence session will be spent brainstorming extemporaneously, it is helpful to encourage people to bring research to the table about the competition and even other industries in regards to these topics. You want to cast as wide a net as possible. That would also include determining if there's any existing input from your customers and your partners.

Opening Mind

Done correctly, Mastermind practices can be a very fruitful way to open minds. Done without thought, they can be frustrating and a waste of time. Whether impromptu or scheduled, they need to have the right mix of freeform thinking and structure in order to result in a productive session. Particularly with C-level executives who tend to have time constraints, a well-structured session can produce more satisfying results. Establishing session roles is also a good idea, even if they are informal. For example, the role of devil's advocate could be played by someone who is not closely attached to the issue or topic. Assigning a facilitator or moderator can help resolve conflicts if they arise, keep the tone of the meeting cordial, and move the conversation along. They can also ensure that all voices are heard and that ideas are captured. The quickest way to kill a Mastermind session is to stifle ideas, ignore inputs by not capturing them, or give the impression that the outcome is already certain.

Keeping Your List

You will want to write down all the ideas that are generated during your Mastermind Intelligence session. Typical options include a whiteboard or large pad on a tripod.

While the latter may be the old-fashioned approach, I favor it because it's more tangible. The pages can be taped to the walls as reminders for later reference and a typed version of the entire list can be emailed to all the attendees at a later date. The ideas can't be erased and forgotten. Perhaps I have been influenced by something Curtis Coy (introduced in Chapter 2) says not just for Mastermind sessions but in terms of management in general: 'Sometimes when your people see you write things down, they tend to pay attention. They tend to follow up. They tend to know that now it's written down and that they'll be held accountable for that. Therefore, I keep a list."[4]

Activating Potential

One of the hardest things to do in a Mastermind practice is to get everyone to participate. There are always those in the room who don't believe they have a voice or have confidence issues and believe their ideas are not worthwhile. The whole point of Mastermind practices is to hear all ideas, no matter how good, bad, silly, or seemingly unfeasible, and then work through them, eliminating them one by one until the group is left with a core few with exceptional potential.

People can be shy at first, so if you want to maximize the value of the time you're spending during a Mastermind Intelligence session, do a pre-meeting warm-up. This exercise will give everyone a bit of practice using their voice in this particular room with these particular people.

If you've ever gone to an improv show where the actors take suggestions from the audience, you've seen this concept before. Pick a simple, low-stakes, wide-open topic and give everyone present the chance to chime in with answers. For example, you could ask people to shout out songs that mention any kind of weather. People could then mention titles (or even lines from songs) such as "*Raindrops Keep Falling on My Head,*" "*Sunny,*" and "*Stormy Weather.*" (If you really want to loosen people up, ask them to sing their answers.)

You can also warm up people's "ideaphoria," a term coined by the Johnson O'Connor Foundation (jocrf.org) that means "the ability to generate ideas." According to Bayer, this is particularly necessary because there will be some individuals in every room who mostly use the analytical side of their brain.

---

[4]Curtis L. Coy, personal communication by recorded telephone interview with the author, December 23, 2013.

"You can't just have ten people who are used to using their rational mind almost exclusively, put them in a room, and say, 'Okay, now be creative.'"

Bayer uses a process he calls "discovery writing" to help systematic-brained thinkers open up their lesser-accessed neural pathways, since they tend to suppress their creativity:

> *The idea is you pick a topic the company is ultimately interested in having some breakthrough around. Let's suppose the goal is to devise a new way of developing some new kind of software to help those in the real estate business. That's the focus. For the next two minutes I would ask everyone in the group to have a pen and a paper and keep their pen moving for two minutes focused on that particular topic. Whatever comes into the mind, they'd be instructed to write down on the paper regardless of the fact that it may have nothing to do with real estate or software. Whatever is in the mind is written down and the pen keeps writing. The pen keeps moving. Those are the two ingredients for the success of this process.*
>
> *The first idea might have something to do with real estate. The second idea might have something to do with new ways of looking at software. The third idea might be, "I can't think of anything else." That's what you'd write down, "I can't think of anything else." The fourth thing is, "Now I'm really frustrated that I can't think of anything else," so you write that down. What this does, especially by keeping the pen moving, is it stops the brain's "editing function." It stops the "judgment function" of the mind and allows it to be free enough to say whatever is there. That safety begins to open up a link or a channel to the creative energies that are deeper within the mind than the editing and judging functions. So out of two minutes, one might only come up sometimes with one decent idea, but that decent idea can then be developed.*

These two steps often make it easier for the team to offer their ideas. But if people still need encouragement, be sure to give it to them. If an idea is rotten, so be it. There are infinite amounts of ideas, and only a handful will be good enough to take to the next level.

I like people to come to a Mastermind Intelligence session bursting with ideas, but it's important for you to guide the conversation so as not to stray too far off course. Ask for attendees to come with a few big ideas already in mind, but don't specify how many. For example, requiring people to bring at least three ideas to the table can feel too structured, especially if you expect them to be ready to fully express them. Then, the group can work together to discuss how or if the ideas fit into overall project goals. There are always some people in the room who are naturally more vocal, and if you ask them for an evaluation of what is being presented, they will usually open up and tell you what they really think.

Staying Open to Outlying Ideas

Many times, organizations fall into familiar patterns as they look for opportunities to innovate. Some people tend to like traditional ideas because they are easier and safer to identify with. Unfortunately, when new ideas are outside of their particular comfort zone, some people may not be open to them. These "outliers" are the very ones that can lead to the greatest innovations, but those with closed or narrow minds are unable to see that.

Make sure you encourage all your attendees to be more willing to consider seemingly "out there" ideas. Bayer offers these suggestions to maximize openness while facilitating a Mastermind Intelligence session:

> Picture a coat checkroom in a nice restaurant during a cold winter. The idea behind the coat checkroom is for diners to identify what is not needed inside the restaurant, like an overcoat or topcoat, and then leave it behind. Like a coat checkroom, a good Mastermind facilitator will encourage everyone participating and present to check their attachments to their own ideas and to their static ways of thinking—to check them at the door, so to speak. . . . Entering the room of the Mastermind session freed and unencumbered by old and familiar ways of thinking enables creativity to truly emerge. It is crucial to not only check our negativity and leave it in the coatroom, but to allow everyone to contribute without judgment. To be without judgment is very important. If a person feels judged, especially in front of a superior, creativity gets squelched. In order for creativity to flow, people need to have a safe environment. The facilitator can create a safe atmosphere by instructing everyone to allow all ideas to be presented without any judgment or criticism.

Often old patterns of caution and hesitancy to share ideas openly block some participants from engaging freely in Mastermind practices. They believe that they should constantly censor themselves.

Bayer also advises to read aloud Mastermind "rules" at the beginning of a session:

> The idea is not only [that you are] not supposed to censor anyone else's ideas, you're not even supposed to censor your own ideas. It is important to remember that creativity springs from a deeper place in one's mind than does that of self-censorship. When we allow the 'editing function' to be checked at the door, we open the channel to the creative energies that exist deeper within the minds of every participant.

Run Meetings with Patience

Every Mastermind session must be run with patience and leadership by example. Start the session by generating all the ideas you possibly can, without any judgment or discussion.

Eventually, it will be time to decide which ideas are worth pursuing in the near term and which should be discarded, at least until the next business wide Mastermind Intelligence session.

In a typical meeting, an idea connects with half of the room almost instantly. This, in turn, may generate interest among everyone else. An idea that has value will quickly gain supporters.

Other times, an idea can get torn apart. When that happens, you have to be careful that the idea itself is being discussed, not the person who presented it. You never want people to feel like they are going to be attacked if they present an unpopular idea. That approach does not encourage open communication.

Sometimes, an idea that bombed in a meeting may actually have some merit, even after the session is over. Ask the person who presented it to spend more time assessing and developing the concept. While the original idea may not be used, often an offshoot of the idea will make far more sense and be much more valuable.

If you still need the confidence to speak out, draw your inspiration from children. Younger thinkers are not yet inhibited by fear of failure or judgment, so they often produce fresher thinking. Even when the idea itself may not be workable in its original form, it may be what is needed to spawn something that does have "legs." Inventions such as popsicles, earmuffs, and trampolines all started out as random musings of children that turned into practical items after more time, thought, and resources had been given to them.

The Next Step

Once you choose the ideas that you want to explore, your next step will be, just as in your Mastermind sessions, to brainstorm different ways to implement them. Eventually, a small group may be assembled to develop a more thorough proposal, but it could be valuable to take advantage of the existing Mastermind group to flesh things out. Someone may come up with a better idea than that generated by a more formal committee.

For example, if in your Mastermind Intelligence session you decide to partner with certain charities around a product launch, the next phase would be to brainstorm different kinds of events or strategies you could implement to make this plan happen. Then, the most popular of those ideas could be worked on by a committee.

An "Asset Strategy" for Your New Project

Once your project is with an official committee, you're past the idea stage. Part of your work going forward will be to come up with an implementation plan. But in order to be operating with your Business Mind, you also need to review as much data as possible to determine if the proposed strategy, which was most likely devised by the intuitive side of the brain, holds water with the analytical side of the brain.

Every vetting process is too different to delve into here. However, the odds are that one or more of the ideas that come from your Mastermind Intelligence session will need to be implemented. Sometimes the most difficult part of a new project is finding the right people to make it happen.

Gary Quinn has an interesting approach to this:

> It doesn't matter what role I have in a project. Based on the vision or strategy I need to implement, the first thing I have to do is look at what I have. What are my assets? When looking at a company, or division, or organization, the biggest challenge, most of the time, is people. Inventorying those people and finding out their capabilities is a challenge.
>
> You've got to get through them one at the time, as best you can. Or you have to have people on your team that you can trust and know how you think. At the same time, you're simultaneously forming or evolving your strategy. Then, you plug in the right people, the assets.
>
> What I tell people to do is draw a picture on the board. Create empty boxes based on different roles you need. Then, go through all your assets and find the best place for them on the board. If necessary, obtain assets you need—put them in the right box. Move them into your organization.

As you're working through this process, call into mind your experiences during the Mastermind Intelligence session with those who stood out as particularly enthusiastic, sensible, or intuitive about the idea now at hand. They might be just who you need now. Your project might be a career changer for them. "A lot of times when reviewing your assets, your people, you ... find out that they're in the wrong box," says Quinn. "Especially if they've been in the company for a while, they may have been moved around and somehow they just got put in a place that's not their strength. So you put them in a different box."

Fostering a Culture of Innovation

Ultimately, Mastermind Intelligence is about more than just creating a new set of ideas and implementation plans; it's about cultivating a company culture where the atmosphere of brainstorming is realized year round. "When you start to feel safe in your job, with your boss, with your department, with your company, with your clients and so forth, then a greater sense of openness of thinking can occur," says Bayer. "You're not just looking to survive. You're looking to thrive. If you're just focusing, like so many people in business do on a daily basis, just on survival in the company . . . your mind gets stuck in very narrow places."

Zak says that creating an environment of trust in an organization should be a priority. "One reason trust is important at work is because it liberates employees to take ownership of projects and be more innovative. If I'm an employee and I think I'm going to get punished if I try something that ultimately fails, then I'm not going to try it. But if I trust my supervisor to support me regardless, then I'm more likely to be more innovative."

He says the best way to create a high-trust organization is to allow for errors, just like you allow the offbeat suggestions that come up in a brainstorming session.

"I sometimes call these 'crowdsourcing mistakes.' You want to have lots of employees doing lots of things. Some things will work better, some things don't."

Most important of all, adds Zak, is your own dependability. "If you're going to build a high-trust organization," he says, "then you, yourself, have to be trustworthy. It starts from the top."

At the same time, Zak says that high trust doesn't mean a lack of intensity. There has to be a mix. He says that places like Google make a practice of hiring quirky, divergent thinkers and elicit innovation by combining high trust with a certain amount of pressure. Trust creates oxytocin in the brain. "As oxytocin increases in the brain," says Zak, "it actually reduces cardiovascular stress. You can actually see this relaxation. In the studies we've done, we've shown that there's a sweet spot between this focused intensity arousal measures in the brain and the sense of relaxation as well. You need both. You need to be 'focus relaxed' or have a 'relaxed focus.' Leaders need to be thinking, 'I don't want to stress you out so much that you're freaked out all the time and you can hardly think. Nor do I want to have you be so underengaged that you're really not putting all your energy into the task at hand.'"

Sweet Spot

Zak says there's a sweet spot where employees are more productive and innovative. "They report more energy when they're in that sweet spot. We have some evidence that they innovate better."

But from a neuroscience standpoint, the brain can't stay in that sweet spot forever. "You need to create an on-and-off switch," he says. "The brain has refractory periods. So you as the leader need to design a challenge, let people work on it and then step back and allow them to reset."

Zak does this by setting project-based goals with obvious finish lines. The scientists who work for him clearly understand whether they've reached the goal or not. When they succeed, there's a celebration in the form of a party, or a day off, plus a bit of breathing room while they ramp up for the next challenge. "It's about helping employees understand that the sweet spot is really a great place to be, but you've also got to step back and give them room to reset."

Mastermind Intelligence Priorities

An implicit feature of a Mastermind Intelligence session is to leave your ego at the door. It's not about you—it's about the company. And the company is about the customers. If you want to implement a Mastermind Intelligence culture that fosters innovation, everyone will place the highest priority on the customer, then the company, then themselves.

Janet Wood, Executive Vice President of Talent and Leadership at SAP, a €16.8B software company, believes this is the right view for any employee to take, although she adds the layer of the team as an extension of the employee[5]:

"You cannot be wrong if the first thing you thought about was 'What's the impact on the customer?'" says Wood. "For me, that really helps put a framework around how to make decisions. My second consideration is the company, or in my case SAP. . . . Then lastly is the team. Sometimes I need to have hard conversations with my team explaining that a decision that is more for the good of the company rather than the good of the team is still the right thing to do."

When Wood was in an organization where the company's products were sold via partners, she changed her focus to the partners. "If our partners are successful, then we know that they are servicing our customers in a way that we encourage," she says. "When I was in charge of global system integrators, our partners were actually delivering the services. My company would sell the software, and then the partners did all of the implementation and business transformation services. So if we are focusing on how we can make our partners the most successful, then by definition, we were also encouraging a better experience for our mutual customers."

---

[5]Janet Wood, personal communication by recorded telephone interview with author, December 18, 2013.

Wood says that thinking this way helps her think strategically. "It helps me feel confident about the decisions I've made," she says, "and I never have to worry about 'Did I put myself or my team ahead of what's best for the customer?'"

Clear Metrics

The organizations I've worked with have found Mastermind Intelligence to be extremely valuable. That's why I'm detailing it here. Weaving Mastermind Intelligence into the heart of your corporate culture is a good idea in theory, but I'm also a strong believer in testing everything to make sure that, even if it works for someone else, it actually works for you.

It can be difficult to determine the impact that discussions of new ideas ultimately have on company performance. However, if you establish clear metrics for evaluating the success of implemented ideas, you will gain a big picture of the value of Mastermind Intelligence practices. Methods for assessing the new projects and offerings include the following:

- Exploring the experiences of similar companies with similar approaches

- Conducting trial runs and measuring results against objectives

- Monitoring what customers are saying about new products and services—for example, via social media

- Analyzing the overall effect on market share

You'll also want to observe employee behavior and morale after major (or minor) company shifts. Plus, new changes could affect people, processes, technology, and information or result in the need for additional employee training. This data should be captured so you know what's working and what might need some improvement.

In the following two chapters, I share engaging exercises to help you recognize key patterns and create strategy maps based on the Four Transformational Intelligences as discussed so far.

Pattern Recognition

Sharpen Your Entire Business Mind

Creativity involves breaking out of established patterns in order to look at things in a different way.

—Edward de Bono

Intelligence is the ability to take in information from the world and to find patterns in that information that allow you to organize your perceptions and understand the external world.

—Brian Greene

The preceding chapters of this book focused on thoughts. You learned about the Four Intelligences and how to orient your mind along those dimensions when thinking about business challenges. The final two chapters of this book are about action—specifically, what you can do to transform your business.

In this chapter, we'll explore pattern recognition as it relates to business transformation and the Four Intelligences. This chapter will provide information on ways for you to think like a detective—recognizing patterns of opportunities and challenges—to capture, interpret, relate, and transform.

Window of Possibilities

So, how can you use pattern recognition to sharpen your focus and alert your business mind to prepare for transformation?

First and foremost, you need to identify patterns that are present in certain events and trends that affect your business. Then, adjust your decisions accordingly. For example, through the application of pattern recognition techniques, you can better understand your customers' thought processes—why and how they buy, what is important to them, how they view you compared to your competition, what influences them, and so on. Once you better understand your customers' minds, you can revisit the steps described in Chapter 3 and improve your Customer Intelligence.

Envision a line connecting your starting point and your targeted goal, with the line going through a window of possibilities, as shown in Figure 6-1. By peering out that window, creative, inspired, and imaginative ideas are in your grasp. However, the window may be foggy, dirty, and even broken at times, obscuring your view.

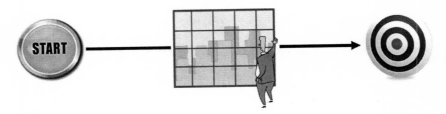

Figure 6-1. Window of possibilities

Your mind is essentially a window of possibilities. It can be creative and innovative, but sometimes it fogs up and must be cleaned by clearing out old views and replacing them with fresh ones. Do you know how to recognize patterns of opportunity and turn your cloudy window into a clear one?

It is easier to make pattern recognition a way of life by observing other people's behavior. For example, let's begin a meeting with ten colleagues by showing them printouts of the following three images:

- Older woman wearing a red business jacket
- Older man wearing a sports jacket
- Red golf ball

Ask each person which two of the three pictures belong together and why. The *why* is key to truly understanding the thought process behind the way your team subconsciously correlates information. Here are different groupings you might hear:

- Woman and man—because of age range
- Woman and man—because of the jacket
- Woman and golf ball—because of the color red
- Man and golf ball—because of sport

You will notice that the focus on which relationships are most important varies greatly. Also observe how people relate to the objects based on their own personal experience or interests. For example, if I like the color red, I might pay more attention to the images of the woman and the golf ball. Sometimes, to learn about your own patterns, you must examine someone else's.

During meetings, notice your colleagues' reactions to new opportunities and note which group they fall into:

1. Protectors—cautious players; point out the potential risks and possible impacts that could occur

2. Optimists—visionaries; willing to explore, take risks, and offer suggestions and solutions

3. Pessimists—naysayers; first thing out of their mouth is "no" until required to act

How about the way they sort information? Do they sort by food, color, people, music, movies, and so on? For example, my mother noticed a while ago that I use restaurants as landmarks when giving directions, which demonstrates a way that I sort pertinent information. Something else I have noticed about myself is that I sort people by astrology signs. I did it for entertainment and conversation's sake when I was much younger, and now it is a subconscious behavior. Everybody has something. It is just how our minds work.

Pay attention to sorting patterns. Remember, be inquisitive but not judgmental with what you observe. What motivates someone and causes their eyes to light up? Hone your observation skills by taking notes and evaluating how you see patterns in others. Then, observe patterns in your own behavior. It doesn't have to be a major discovery. It could be something small, like noticing that you tend to be more proactive in the mornings than in the afternoons. Try to spend some time each day in reflective thought on looking for patterns, making it a habit that readily comes to you. The activity will shift from your conscious mind to your subconscious mind, which is the goal.

Recognizing Patterns

Why is it that some people miss opportunities that are right in front of them, whereas others recognize them immediately and take action?

Generally, the latter are positive go-getters, with a "let's see what is possible" mentality and can-do attitude. They attract possibilities and opportunities. These are people that have trained their brains to notice patterns and opportunities, perhaps unconsciously, through repeated focus and awareness.

When preparing to transform a business, look for patterns prior to beginning that could help you determine which actions to take. These patterns may be within your business, or they may occur outside of it. Train your brain to scan for possibilities brought on by external changes. As we discussed, constant repetition will create an unconscious habit so that eventually you will be doing this without even being aware of it. Start by taking notice of what has changed outside of your business. Is there a pattern to this activity? What are the media and industry analysts paying attention to? What trends are happening?

Then, note the patterns that are occurring *inside* your business. Perhaps you'll notice a pattern in the demands your customers are making. Go through your customer support feedback. What are customers asking for? Is it something you can support, change, or alter? Do you notice a direct correlation between what your customers are asking for and what is happening in the market? Sometimes there's a clear-cut pattern, but plenty of times there isn't.

Consider how the online flower order service developed. A number of factors paved the way for this opportunity:

- Increased demands in work and lifestyles led to lack of time for friends and family

- Vast increase in the number of personal computers

- Development of software that could track customer information, including key event reminders, such as birthdays and anniversaries

- Creation of mechanisms to transmit secure financial details over the Internet

The flower shop industry didn't notice these patterns all at once, but gradually, over time. Business decision makers often recognize one or two variables at a time that eventually lead to a solid, actionable pattern. Comments like,

"I think I might have something" or "There is something there, but I am not quite sure what" should trigger further investigation. Customer complaints can also fall into that category, such as the following:

- 5:00 PM closing times at flower shops doesn't give customers enough time to get to the shop after work.

- Customers are not satisfied since they can't actually see what they ordered over the phone.

- There is often miscommunication about orders, delivery dates, and recipient addresses.

As you can discern from the sample complaints above, connections may be made one at a time, while unfolding into an overarching pattern. This pattern can be shaped into a realized action plan, thanks to time, teamwork, open minds, and creativity.

Unfog the Window of Possibilities That Leads to Transformation

Due to the cloudiness of their perception, people do not always fully realize all of the facets of a possibility. Recall the concept represented by Figure 6-1. You may view possibilities out of your window, but unless your focus is clear, you will leave opportunities on the proverbial table. Work to uncover as much information as possible, and then evaluate, refine, and redirect. The process is never complete and continues to evolve. This is how businesses transform. For example, the floral industry looked for opportunities to up-sell and subsequently began selling chocolates, stuffed animals, balloons, gift baskets, and more. They then partnered with or acquired complementary companies and made deals with shipping companies and local florists to expand their reach. But, it won't stop there. They can look into loyalty reward programs, create mobile apps for ease of ordering, and use social media to drive more traffic and sales.

As opportunity assessments are conducted and information is uncovered on the path to transformation, business leaders must allow flexibility when the need arises to veer from the path in order to maximize possibilities.

Identify, Observe, Examine, and Assess

As we've discussed, it can be easier to recognize patterns in others before you can recognize them in yourself. If you're married, just think about the patterns you've observed in your spouse, and vice versa. This also holds true when identifying business patterns, both internally and externally.

There are three main steps to follow when employing pattern recognition to transform your business:

1. Identify external events and trends. Start by taking note of events and trends happening outside of your company. Think about key changes in technology, markets, demographics, and other relevant areas. Also, think about your team's social connections. Has your network been growing at a good pace? The more people you have relationships with, the more opportunities you can identify. Don't forget to ask your business partners what external events and trends they are noticing—and if they are acting on any.

2. Observe internal patterns of issues and complaints. Are there issues that come up again and again? Is there any relationship between the types of complaints and issues that are happening? What is the root cause? What areas need your attention?

3. Examine and assess any links between seemingly unrelated events or trends. Are there any dots between steps 1 and 2 that you might be able to connect?

These steps, however, are not definitive. Sometimes an individual or team recognizes an internal pattern before identifying an external event or trend. If you are starting from scratch, however, these steps are useful to follow.

Leverage Your Human Assets

Everyone on your team has a different background. When you are looking for patterns, particularly external to your company, make use of whatever extra knowledge or context your team members can provide. For example, perhaps someone on your team has experience in the legal field. Leverage these special skills by encouraging this individual to focus on aspects on the project relating to legal affairs. That extra input could be the difference in turning an identified opportunity into a realized goal.

A "dream team" with a broad range of experience can also bring greater value when recognizing patterns and assessing opportunities. The broader the knowledge, the greater the chances to connect the dots between events or trends, especially those that are not easily noticeable.

Jumping to Conclusions

Nothing is more frustrating than being on the phone with a customer service representative who is not truly listening to your concerns. He might interrupt you midsentence with a quick-fix solution to the issue he assumes you have, when your problem is something else entirely. You may then think he is rude and impatient. But why do some service representatives have poor listening skills?

As I mentioned in Chapter I, the neocortex part of our brain predicts what we will encounter based on data it has previously captured through our various senses. This information leads us to automatically assume what will occur in the future. The brains of many people you communicate with are constantly in preparation mode, predicting what you are going to say and do next. That is why the customer service representative interrupted you. He assumed to know your question based on patterns that his neocortex recognized. These patterns take the form of keywords and phrases that you use when you call in, such as "I am having trouble logging in." Based on that phrase, the customer service representative might assume you have forgotten your password, which may or may not be the case.

Your brain does the very same thing when looking for possibilities or facing new situations. It makes assumptions based on prior experiences. It makes judgments about a pattern that has been recognized. That judgment or assumption could be entirely wrong, but the brain is trained to relate new information to that captured by your past experiences. When dealing with large amounts of data, the brain jumps to conclusions quickly.

If you are alert to the fact that your mind is likely to make unproven assumptions, you can train yourself to slow down and be aware when it happens. Here's how:

1. Take your time when reviewing data.

2. Notice when you are making an assumption. Write it down.

3. Ask yourself, "Is this true? Does the material I'm looking at right now really support this assumption, or am I referring to an experience from the past?"

4. Ask yourself, "Are there other possible meanings here that I may be ignoring when I make this assumption?"

5. Look at the data again and see if you notice something different.

Focus Requires Balance

There is a balancing component to effective focus. When you focus too much on one thing, you may miss other opportunities. The key is to focus on your target while simultaneously keeping an open mind.

Also, when your focus is too intense, you tend to feel stress. Focusing on the outcome is good, but give yourself space for spontaneous ideas that may offer a different path to your outcome. A softer focus will make it easier for creativity and innovation to emerge. Make sure that your confidence in knowing what you want is balanced by your comfort in not being exactly sure how to get there. Success often comes when you make room for "not knowing."

To bring about true transformation, you must garner the support of your subconscious mind. You need a vision of the outcome to energize your mind and body so you can propel yourself in the direction of change. You can achieve what you want more easily, effortlessly, and less stressfully when your conscious and subconscious mind work together toward a common goal.

Stumbling on Ideas

Looking for the next big opportunity shouldn't be stressful. The key is to take small steps, possibly starting with a little hop. You most likely will stumble on something you never imagined before you got started on your journey. This unexpected stumbling often turns out to lead to the most wonderful transformative possibilities for your business. All you have to do is be alert and have an open mind while you're searching. This is the way people stumble onto ideas.

Small and Manageable

Make sure not to put too much pressure on yourself and your team to find the next big thing. The small possibilities are often the ones that make the biggest impact. Don't rule out smaller scale opportunities that are more manageable and can be implemented in a shorter time period. Implementation requires resources, funds, and time. Also, when we postpone or delay smaller opportunities while trying to implement larger ones, other factors may change. For example, a bigger opportunity may only be fully implemented three years after the initial pattern was identified. Within that time period, a lot can change, potentially negating some of the value of the original opportunity. Start small and build incrementally.

For example, let's revisit our small florist. Pretend our small shop is currently mailing out catalogs that showcase beautiful floral arrangement designs. But, some of the flower arrangements might be discontinued or unavailable by the time a customer decides to call and place a phone order, leading to customer dissatisfaction. A way to remedy this problem is for the florist to go from a catalog-based business to a web-based business, which can handle requests and update product information in real time. Realistically though, this is a huge goal that could be a few years off. Instead, florists could begin by experimenting with a simple, informational web site about the availability of various floral arrangements. They can progress to a transactional web site that would include a shopping cart and order tracking. This would allow them to test the site, work out the kinks, and then continue to the next possibility.

Delta of Possibilities

Let's envision that you and your team have used your business minds to identify an exciting opportunity. Now you want to assess if it makes sense for your business to take the plunge and pursue it.

Start by evaluating your current state and then determine what your target is. The difference between the two is your "delta of possibilities." Picture again the window of possibilities in Figure 6-1. Prepare to look through this window—assess and analyze if the possibility is doable.

Using the lens of the Four Intelligences, we could see our humble florist's current state as being hallmarked by the following:

- Financial Intelligence > Declining Revenue
- Customer Intelligence > Order Complaints
- Data Intelligence > Lack of Order Tracking System
- Mastermind Intelligence > Miscommunication; Lack of Training and Motivation

Using the same view, the florist's targeted goals could be the following:

- Financial Intelligence > Increased Revenue
- Customer Intelligence > Web-Ordering Mechanism; Customer Satisfaction
- Data Intelligence > Online Order Tracking System
- Mastermind Intelligence > Increase in Productivity; Alert and Focused

To reach the desired targets, you must work backward using the Four Intelligences. For example, you could work on the issue of internal miscommunication first. What is it going to take to turn things around so that communication is a positive experience? Using Mastermind Intelligence, engage your employees and your team to look for creative solutions.

From there, use similar Mastermind Intelligence techniques to tackle the lack of an order tracking system. You'll note that there are lots of synergies to be realized among your various goals. Implementation of an order tracking system would also improve your Data Intelligence. Then, switch to Customer Intelligence needs. What do your customers need? Use these insights to put together a web-interfacing ordering application that will improve customer satisfaction. Next, set up a process to track the data you need to measure progress against your goal of increased revenue. This step falls under the umbrella of Financial Intelligence. To help you visually encode this process, I have drawn out an image of showing where you currently are (Step #1), the action process phase (Step #2), and the target (Step #3), shown in Figure 6-2.

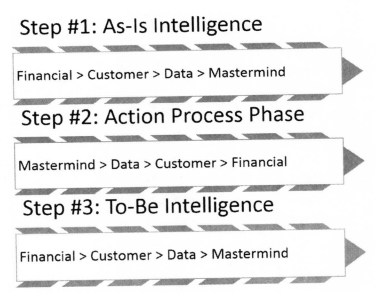

Figure 6-2. Current, action, target

Advanced Pattern Recognition Techniques

Businesses can also use data-modeling and data-mining techniques to recognize patterns within large sets of data. This is beneficial when identified opportunities involve big data and predictive analytics. Data modeling can provide visuals about the organization's data, and it allows for collaboration across the enterprise. It is also a helpful tool to use when working on service level agreements (SLAs) by painting a picture of what data currently exists and where. It also provides a glimpse into what data is missing and what data is needed, for planning purposes.

In Chapter 4, we discussed the need to create universal, clear definitions of various data across an organization and then ensure that these definitions are shared and encoded throughout the company through training and repetition. To take that concept further, metadata is data about the data or information about the information. It's confusing, I know. Think of it as a professional bio for your data, capturing key facts such as who can access it, who owns it, who uses it, and where it comes from. Management of metadata information can be found in a data model tool. This is particularly helpful when addressing governance, security, risk, compliance, audit, and legal concerns because it ensures that all your ducks are in a row.

Intelligence Hub

Use the intelligence hub discussed in Chapter 4 to centrally manage governance, risk, and compliance. In other words, designate a central location in your organization to oversee major transformational activities. From a bird's eye view, the hub can manage any potential, unintended impacts your project may have in another area of the organization. For example, if you are transforming the HR department, an intelligence hub would cross-check to make sure there is no impact in the finance or marketing department.

The intelligence hub houses the unified definitions, processes, and enterprise wide data oversight functions, and it functions as the central repository of information flow. The mission of the intelligence hub is to make sure the company's vision, strategies, plans, and processes work in harmony. For example, a centralized view of governance practices allows for effective and efficient management of performance, as well as awareness of risk and compliance.

Transformational Strategy

Patterns are around us every day. Once you learn to open your mind and recognize patterns, you will then be able to determine how to make patterns contribute to the success of your business. You will also recognize the need to train your brain to explore the possibilities identified by your newfound skill and ensure the "Window of Possibilities" in your mind is crystal clear, clean, and wide open to whatever is out there.

Strategy Mapping

Integrating the Four Intelligences into Your Business

Strategy is a pattern in a stream of decisions.

—Henry Mintzberg, McGill University

What's the use of measuring speed if you don't go in the right direction?

—Jeroen De Flander

I hope at this point in the book your wheels are turning and you're beginning to ponder the opportunities using the Four Intelligences in your own company. After determining your destination (that is, your strategy), you then need to program the GPS or your navigation system (strategy map) to get there as smoothly as possible.

However, the art of strategy mapping is more than just improving performance; it must involve doing things differently. A well thought-out map empowers many people, not only leaders, to use the data to effect change. This chapter will guide you in the creation of strategy maps for your own organization. Strategy maps devised following this process will also help you identify any key data or patterns overlooked earlier in your opportunity development process.

Strategy Mapping

Strategy maps set metrics and key performance indicators (KPIs) that indicate how an organization is performing against strategic goals and objectives, as well as in relation to the overall vision and strategy of an organization.

Businesses using the Four Intelligences actively collect and monitor relevant data about their processes in order to make informed decisions. The Four Intelligences also help position decision makers to swiftly respond to changes in markets, competitors, trends, and customers. Most people equate success with receiving mountains of data, but this notion is wrong. Success is about having the right data—balanced data that is focused on the areas your organization is looking to improve. The data output from the Four Intelligences becomes the data input for the strategy map, as shown in Figure 7-1.

Figure 7-1. Data output of the Four Intelligences becomes data input for the strategy map

Strategy mapping using output from the Four Intelligences allows for the following:

- Financial goals to be met
- Customer satisfaction and loyalty
- Data and visual insight into the organization
- Mastermind-level empowerment and creativity

Ingredients of a Strategy Map

As we know, life isn't all about opportunities. It's often about challenges. We must face challenges in the same way that we face opportunities. The intent is to find solutions. Using the Four Intelligences, your organization can also find solutions to challenges by using a strategy map. Figure 7-2 shows you the key ingredients of a strategy map.

Figure 7-2. Strategy map ingredients

If the map seems daunting, don't worry. You have the ingredients already in your cupboard, as they are the outputs from the Four Intelligences. These data outputs will then become the inputs for your strategy map. Let's take a closer look at each one.

#1—Strategic Objective

Strategic objectives are derived from the vision and strategy of the organization. The purpose of including these objectives in a strategy map is to redirect the organization from the tyranny of maintaining the status quo with only slight improvements here and there. If an organization does not constantly change, it is at risk because its competitors might offer similar products or services. In short, strategic objectives define the changes an organization should make to maintain a competitive edge.

Everyone in the company must understand the overall corporate goals and objectives and how each specific job relates to achieving them. Companies need to communicate down through the organization when setting goals and objectives.

As part of this exercise, make sure to establish a responsibility matrix or a RACI (Responsible, Accountable, Consulted, and Informed) diagram for each objective. Understand the roles of the assignees and involved parties by answering these questions:

- Who is **responsible** for working on the activity and making sure the job is done correctly?

- Who has ultimate **accountability** and decision-making authority for managing and ensuring success of the initiative or project?

- Who must be **consulted** when making decisions and taking action?

- Who needs to be **informed** of a decision or action, and when?

Figure 7-3 demonstrates a sample RACI matrix.

Activity	Executive Sponsor	Project Manager	Business Analyst	Key User
Confirm Purpose	Responsible / Accountable	Responsible	Consulted	Informed
Define Objectives	Consulted	Responsible / Accountable	Consulted	Informed
Develop Approach	Consulted / Informed	Responsible / Accountable	Responsible / Consulted	Informed
Prepare Requirements	Informed	Responsible / Informed	Consulted	Informed
Identify As-Is	Informed	Responsible / Informed	Consulted / Informed	Consulted / Informed

Figure 7-3. Sample RACI matrix

If you are using a system to track and document your strategy map, like the one shown in Figure 7-4, make sure that it includes assignees and all related parties. Assignees are those assigned to execute a strategic objective or initiative and are generally your staff. For example, corporate compliance might need participation from finance, general counsel, and paralegals. These participants could be defined as those individuals who are responsible and/or accountable, based on the RACI matrix.

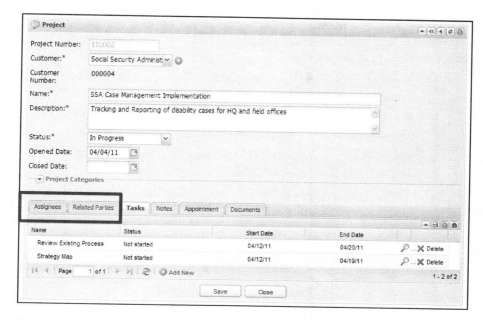

Figure 7-4. Example of a strategy map tracking system, including assigned and related parties

Involved parties may be external or internal to the organization. Examples of external parties could be contractors, subject matter experts, or auditors. Internal parties may consist of steering committee members, human resources, or marketing. In summary, an involved party can be defined as anyone who is consulted or informed based on the RACI matrix.

#2—Set Priorities

Setting priorities should be done on a consistent basis. Some people might order priorities based on what they can finish the most quickly. Others may choose items that use the fewer number of resources or require the least risk.

Just as you created universal definitions of data, you must also create definitions when setting priorities. To apply a formal approach to prioritization, it is helpful to perform a SWOT (Strength, Weakness, Opportunity, and Threat) analysis. Opportunities are external, while strength is internal. Try to find the balance of your greatest strength/opportunity with your realized weaknesses and present threats and set priorities accordingly.

Imagine you have two objectives at a given time:

1. Consolidation of two departments, such as HR and Legal

2. Establishment of financial compliance for entry on the New York Stock Exchange

Which objective should you place as highest priority? In order to determine this, a SWOT analysis is essential, as shown in Figure 7-5. The following questions will guide your analysis:

- Strength (internal): Do I already have best practices and framework established elsewhere that can be reused?

- Weakness (internal): Do I have the necessary resources and skills available internally or do I need to outsource?

- Opportunity (external): Will this benefit our customers and drive more business?

- Threat (external): Is there a factor driving this such as an audit, competition, or a legal mandate?

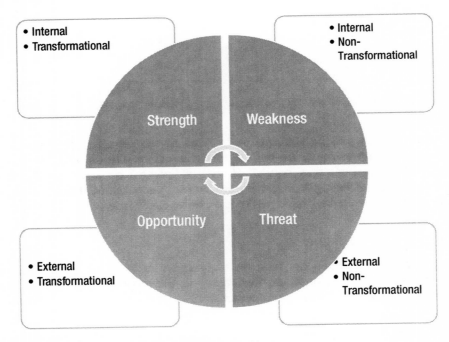

Figure 7-5. Using SWOT to help determine priorities

It is important to keep in mind that actions taken to address a weakness or threat are non-transformative, while objectives based on strengths or opportunities are transformative in nature.

#3—Measures, Metrics, and KPIs

Let's start with a quick, broad definition of each of these three terms:

- **Measure:** A one-time sum such as the number of employees you hired in January

- **Metric:** Two or more measurements, often over a period of time, such as the number of employees you hired per month during the fiscal calendar year

- **Key Performance Indicator (KPI):** A comparison, usually compared to a target, such as your targeted goal for new employees during the fiscal calendar year compared to the number of employees you actually hired

When establishing measures, metrics, and KPIs, it is important to have common definitions of these terms across the team or the organization. Imagine tracking performance when there is not a unified definition of what is being measured. Each company is different and, therefore, you should select measures, metrics, and KPIs that are appropriate for you.

Another point of confusion within organizations is the difference between a metric and KPI. Although I covered it in the first part of this book, let's make things clearer using an example of plastic surgeons.

Plastic surgeons have their own metrics to measure their business success:

- Total number of patients
- Total number of satisfied patients
- Total number of repeat patients
- Total number of referrals

The KPIs that plastic surgeons might track could be the total number of patient appointments as a result of the following:

- Advertisements in magazines
- Mentions on *The Oprah Winfrey Show* or *The Dr. Oz Show*
- Plastic surgeon's newly published book

The key to appropriately defining measures, metrics, and KPIs is to capture the right data and to present it in terms that are relevant to your business. Then, you need to communicate and translate the data into a meaningful and useful language so that all parties can relate to it no matter what department they may be in or role they might have.

Once you have determined what measures, metrics, and KPIs you will be using for your business, here's what else you have to do:

- Document your definitions, formulae, and unit types for each of these items

- Communicate each of these items to everyone involved

- Get feedback to ensure everyone understands your definitions and can work with your parameters

- Make any necessary changes after getting feedback

For example, a typical cluster of project-related metrics might include these elements:

- Metric Name: percentage of active projects on time

- Metric Definition: percentage of projects performed within the planned timeframe per baseline

- Metric Formula: percentage of number of active projects delivered on time based on total number of active projects

- Metric Unit Type: percentage

If clear definitions are not established, decisions makers will not be able to reliably report whether their company is making progress in areas of importance to the board of directors, shareholders, customers, employees, and the community at large. Sometimes an outside consultant is needed to help identify, define, and bring synergy to your measures, metrics, and KPIs.

#4—Data Sources

Do you have an enterprise-wide view of all your data sources?

If your objective or initiative is related to data consolidation across departments or the organization, then you might be integrating disparate data sources. You need to understand where data are coming from. If you must synchronize data from different systems that use different formats, field names, or data characteristics, you need to ensure that you have consistent data sources for your application systems.

Data modeling can help you to interpret and understand the data sources, data types, and data locations to include in your strategy map. It will also let you know where to look if the need to modify, create, and/or manage data arises.

#5—SLA Targets

With any new or revised strategic objective, establishing a formal service level agreement (SLA) is significant. It brings parties together to share, brainstorm, and document appropriate expectations. Best of all, it helps establish targets. Targets are critical in bringing focus and clarity so that an organization can make improvements. A target, if communicated appropriately, can be used as a motivational and positive reinforcement technique. Make sure everyone agrees on the targets and expected performance. You could even use a red, yellow, and green dashboard, for example, to track your team's progress in reaching your target based on actual values against the targeted values. This allows you to periodically check the status to make necessary adjustments as needed.

The formality of an SLA should be looked at as a means of communication, not a method for penalizing or measuring someone's performance. It should reflect the discussions that occur among the staff, managers, and executives, followed by the expectations and negotiated points set among internal departments and/or between internal and external parties. Drawing up a formal SLA brings attention to issues and lessons learned, and it also increases the probability for consistent improvements to occur while expected service levels are being addressed.

Having a formal SLA also sets a level of priority and understanding for the provider, based on what is of most importance to the client. Formalizing the SLA alleviates fear and assures the business units and clients that their strategic and tactical objectives will be met.

For an external service provider, the penalty clause within an SLA is an incentive to maintain a certain level of service; otherwise, there is financial liability. If the provider fails to meet the outlined service level requirements, they must compensate the client accordingly. However, not all penalty clauses include financial punitive measures to mitigate the lack of SLA requirements, which makes it critically important to outline and negotiate specific details within the SLA that all parties can agree to and reasonably meet. A formal SLA creates a professional business relationship with the client, even if they are internal, thus creating a more productive environment.

Preparing for Formal SLAs

There are several considerations when preparing formal SLAs. The following are the main ones to explore:

- **Executive Sponsorship:** Make sure there is an executive sponsor involved if you are not one. It is up to executive leadership, executive sponsors, and senior management to stress the importance of formal internal SLAs. As the sponsor, you need to help paint the bigger picture, emphasizing that the SLA improves communication and that it is not a method to measure performance.

- *Involve the Appropriate Parties:* Make sure you identify and bring all parties involved to the table so that the business, technical, and legal perspectives are considered. SLAs are not just for IT—SLAs can be for the financial, HR, sales, marketing, and other departments. In addition to involving the legal department, some organizations need to involve the administrative teams as well. Make sure to involve day-to-day supervisory management staff that will be directly affected by the performance standards established with the SLA requirements; they are best able to provide input based on their roles.

- *Review Strategic Objectives:* It is best when the strategic objective of the organization is reviewed with the team so that everyone understands the goals and mission. Again, connect and coordinate. If there are any current measures, metrics, and KPIs being used, bring those to the table to be discussed. Note that IT service metrics will be different from HR, financial, and other metrics. In addition, consider new metrics based on what others in your industry are doing in a similar environment. You want to make sure there is not an overload of metrics being captured, but a sufficient amount to fulfill the business objective.

- *Apply to Executive Needs (Higher Picture):* When gathering requirements for a formal SLA, it is best to link it to a performance management improvement project in order to evaluate which metrics are important for the executive when he or she makes business decisions. If you find that the necessary information is not being captured, you will better be able to evaluate your data governance needs and requirements.

- *Duration and Review Timeline:* SLAs should have an established term. It is also best to reevaluate an SLA at a set interval, or during the budgeting process for the coming year, to determine commitment levels and budgets, if applicable. The agreements will change as demands and requirements change (new policies, new processes, new mandates and regulations that need to be met, and so on).

- *Don't Create an Issue out of a Non-Issue:* When gathering SLA requirements, make sure you don't create an issue out of a non-issue. For example, if scheduled downtime is not important, don't include it as part of the SLA. Address the real problem areas where there is a need for process improvement. Be cautious not to overmeasure. Stay focused on the target.

#6—Internal and External Data

Review your internal and external data against your strategic objectives. Brainstorm and discuss these questions:

- What data is being captured?

- What data is missing, and how can you get it?

- What data is obsolete? What will you do with it while remaining compliant with internal or external monitoring organizations? Will you store it, purge it, or delete it?

- What data is being captured by the marketplace and your competitors?

- What external factors could impact this initiative? These factors could be anything from unemployment rates to gas prices to the housing market, as well as any market trends.

Take Action!

As we move to the final section of this book, I want to encourage you to take action and create one simple strategy map as part of your day-to-day work/life activity. In doing so, you will start to form a habit that will impact your next major business transformation opportunity.

Your practice strategy maps should be based on one simple strategic goal of your choosing, highlighting two or three metrics and KPIs, targets, and possible external data to be captured. Over time, you will draft additional versions of more complex strategy mappings. But for now, at least, walk through the steps for one general strategic objective with a small group or team.

Step 1—Gather and Organize

Use elicitation techniques to understand and capture requirements such as surveys, interviews, shadowing, brainstorming, or analysis of existing documents.

Step 2—Analyze and Validate

In order to ensure quality and integrity of your input, analyze and validate the data you have collected. Link back and check to see if the method for obtaining the data makes sense and fulfills the purpose of the strategic objective. I once had a data architect tell me that the data source of a metric came from a PowerPoint he had received. That made me question his credibility as a data architect. I then pointed out that the PowerPoint content was based on data derived from "elsewhere" and asked him to identify exactly where that "elsewhere" was.

As shown in Figure 7-6, the data you collected then becomes the input for your strategy map. When analyzing and validating data, assess the impacts on other projects or initiatives.

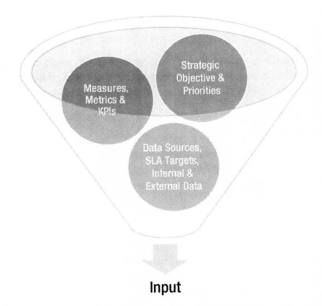

Figure 7-6. Data elicited during Step 1 becomes the input for strategy mapping

Step 3—Collaborate and Communicate

Next, input the data from each of the Four Transformational Intelligences into the strategy map, as shown in Figure 7-7. Then, communicate and collaborate accordingly with your team.

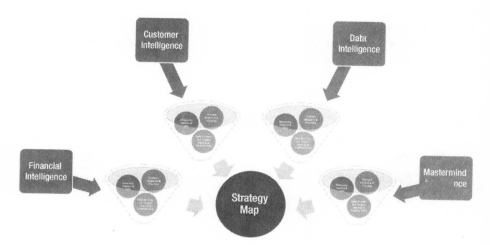

Figure 7-7. Using the Four Intelligences to form a strategy map

What are your department's best practices for staying engaged with the rest of your organization so that both the department and company can be mutually responsive to each other's needs? At this point in the process, use the assignees and parties identified in the RACI matrix to communicate and collaborate. Confirm that everyone agrees that the targets are achievable and can realistically be performed. It is important at this step to have agreement and approval on targets before you move on.

Step 4—Document and Relate

Now that you have confirmation and approval, it is time to document and link the data captured together. A typical strategy map template may be conveniently broken down into seven columns, as follows:

- Column 1—Insert the strategic objective for each Intelligence
- Column 2—Set and organize priorities
- Column 3—Include measures, metrics, and KPIs
- Column 4—Identify data sources
- Column 5—Insert agreed target levels
- Column 6—Examine the results of internal and external data

A seventh column might be titled "Strategic Initiative/Action." These column heads serve as action programs or ways to achieve the targets. You then write down the findings that will enable you to meet the target for a specific strategic objective in the columns. For example, the end result could be that the company should make a specific investment or launch a certain marketing campaign. This is actionable activity. Sometimes these actionable activities can become another strategic objective.

Cause-and-Effect Relationships

Once you create your strategy map, you then link, or relate, it to a strategic initiative and its actionable activities. For example, look at the strategic initiative for a hotel sorted by the Four Intelligences:

- Financial Intelligence > Action is to grow revenues
- Customer Intelligence > Action is to increase quality of customer experience
- Data Intelligence > Action is to improve technology systems
- Mastermind Intelligence > Action is to enhance employee processes

You then can link the Four Transformational Intelligences together based on your results from the strategy map, as show in Table 7-1, and you use your business mind to determine reasonable action steps to take based on the strategic initiatives. Now loop back and apply the Four Transformational Intelligences.

Table 7-1. Linking Four Intelligences Together Based on Results from Strategy Mapping

Intelligences	Strategic Initiative / Action	Reasonable Activities
Financial Intelligence	Grow Revenues	Establish ROI (Marketing, Technology, Services, Training)
Customer Intelligence	Increase Quality of Customer Experience	Gain Repeat Customer / Generate Word-of-Mouth Marketing
Data Intelligence	Improve Technology Systems and Services	Improve Check-In & Check-Out Systems, Enhance Mattresses, Offer Complimentary Shuttle Service, and Free Wi-Fi
Mastermind Intelligence	Enhance Employee Processes	Enrich Reservation Process, Hospitality Training, Memorable Experience for Guests

You can see from Table 7-1 that if a hotel's financial initiative is to grow revenues, one way they can do this is to invest in activities to increase the quality of the customer experience. This investment will gain repeat customers and generate positive word-of-mouth publicity. In order to perform this Customer Intelligence strategic initiative, the hotel must invest in better check-in and check-out systems, new and upgraded mattresses, complimentary shuttle services, and advanced technology services for guests (free Wi-Fi connections and movies on demand). To accomplish all of those tasks, innovative and creative employees are needed to drive the input. For the target of enriching the reservation process, hospitality training should strive to make a memorable experience for guests, creating the need for innovation.

A state university provides another example. A state university generally focuses on growth of student enrollment and the number of programs offered. These growth calculations are reflected annually or biannually in state funding formulas. State funds are then used to stimulate and support new programs and new facilities. Based on this information, what are some examples of reasonable activities you could come up with to transform a state university? In Table 7-2, I share some examples of targets to increase enrollment.

Table 7-2. Increase Enrollment to Attract and Gain State Funds for the University

Strategic Objective = Have New Programs and New Facilities	
Intelligences	**Reasonable Activities**
Financial Intelligence	Increase Number of Freshman Applicants and Sophomore Transfers
Customer Intelligence	Marketing & PR Announcement about Internship Programs and Credits, High Rates of Hire Prior to Graduation
Data Intelligence	Enhance Career Path Programs / Create Links between Universities and Job Fairs
Mastermind Intelligence	Motivate Faculty to Finding Business Partners to Hire for Educational Internship Paid or Credit

Now let's assume you work for the state university, which has a wonderful dance department. To increase enrollment, you launch a marketing campaign about the dance program and include famous dancers who are alumni. You feel this will be effective since you've noticed a spike in interest in dance as a result of TV shows such as *Dancing with the Stars* and *So You Think You Can Dance?* You then track the campaign's effectiveness using KPIs to see how many students enroll in the university's dance program because of these marketplace changes. As a result of the success of this campaign, another strategic objective is created to implement big data within the university. The intention of big data is to predict areas of interest, determine enrollment peaks, and identify other trends that drive short-term marketing campaigns.

Looking Forward and Backward

There is constant, interrelated assessment, review, and analysis taking place among the Four Intelligences. Many times, you can improve initiatives by looking forward and backward, as shown in Figure 7-8.

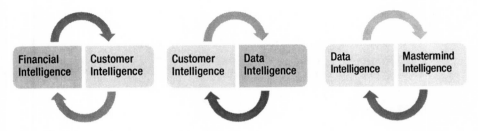

Figure 7-8. Looking forward and backward

Going back to our hotel example, if you were to work backward and start with Mastermind Intelligence, you might find ways to improve the current strategic goals and objective, as shown in Figure 7-9.

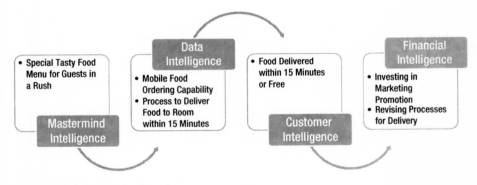

Figure 7-9. Working backward

Monitor and Refine

Monitor and observe both internal and external patterns. What can be changed or modified? What needs to be improved? What's working? What's not?

As you modify or change your strategy map, do so incrementally. Don't try to create anything from scratch or recreate strategy maps for the entire organization at once. Small steps can have big impacts. Start by refining one step, and then expand and take two or more steps. Keep in mind that a strategy map is not a fixed plan. It is an ongoing journey that helps guide the transformation of the business.

If you decide to use a strategy map tracking system, make sure it has a dashboard so you can easily see your top three to five metrics and/or KPIs. This will help you notice and modify patterns and also help you identify the root cause of issues that arise. A dashboard might, for example, address simple project-related metrics such as the following:

- Number of open projects
- Number of open tasks
- Number of critical alerts
- Number of in-progress statuses

The Output of a Strategy Map

A strategy map helps you define what you need, when you need it, and how you are going to achieve it. How do you know if your organization needs big data without implementing a strategy map? The same is true for cloud computing, mobility, outsourcing, software-as-a-service (SaaS), web intelligence, and much more. Often we purchase and apply what we think is a solution without analyzing what the actual issue is that we're trying to solve. It is like taking an aspirin to ease your headache even though your headache may be the result of caffeine withdrawal, a brain tumor, or another medical condition. Regardless of the issue, that aspirin could only be a temporary fix until a doctor provides you with a proper diagnosis.

A strategy map will continually help you solve the problems you are actually trying to solve because it is a dynamic, ever-changing tool. Executives using strategy maps can adeptly shift directions based on new insights and observations.

Also, the output of a strategy map is used as the input for the following:

- Gap analysis
- Project implementation
- Preparation for governance, risk management, compliance (GRC), and legal matters
- Framework and certification planning such as Data Governance, ITIL, Six Sigma, and Lean
- Reporting tools such as scoreboards and dashboards

Remember to revisit the beginning of this book, review your thoughts, and apply the Four Transformational Intelligences to other areas of your business. You now know how to use your business mindset and find patterns to make lasting, impactful changes.

Evaluation

I use five criteria to evaluate the success of an approved strategy map. You can use these criteria to evaluate an already created strategy map, or you can evaluate it while you are still in the process of implementing it:

1. Is the target being met? Did the result provide the expected planned outcome?

2. Is the organization able to maintain or enhance the mapped strategy over a period of time, or does it need to retract?

3. Are all parties, both those who created the map and those involved in its implementation, enthusiastic and positive about the long-term potential?

4. Does the strategy map complement other strategic goals of the organization?

5. Is the strategy map flexible enough to be modified or refined?

Use these criteria or develop additional ones as you see fit for your organization.

Frequently Asked Questions (FAQ)

Q: How do you define a successful strategy map?

- A: Before you can measure success, you must have a clear vision of what constitutes success in your organization and your industry. Compare the identity and reputation of your organization with that of the overall marketplace and your competitors.

Q: How should these strategy maps be executed to help the organization reach its targets?

- A: Choose the most important measures, metrics, KPIs, and targets to achieve. Establish the best possible team to help execute. Communicate the strategic initiative and actionable items effectively with the team. Help ensure targets will be met in a controlled manner so as not to overwhelm the team. Be sensitive to industry trends, competition, the marketplace, and external factors when deciding to invest time, money, and resources. Have a manageable document tracking or system in place to help you evaluate progress and notice patterns.

Q: What should each department or division do to accomplish approved targets?

- A: In order to move toward a declared target, make sure all the assignees, involved parties, and key decision makers understand the strategy map, strategic initiatives, action-able activities, and expectations. Be flexible and ready to change, modify, and refine these things if necessary.

Key Takeaway You will never be able to measure every parameter for every area your organization is involved in. Instead, focus on key areas and set targets that are appropriate, given the internal and external data provided at that given time.

As You Continue On Your Journey

To be a transformational leader, consult this book whenever you approach new projects, objectives, and initiatives and activate your leadership on three interlocking and dynamically interacting fronts:

- understand (consulting the first five chapters on your business mind).

- do (consulting the final two chapters on transformational action informed by knowledge of your business mind).

- evolve (by mindful practice). By noticing patterns, and recognizing different intelligences, you will start to do so subconsciously and you will find them everywhere—in your business, customers, partners, and social interactions.

Become...so you can answer the two questions posed at the beginning of this book without hesitation:

- How confident am I that my business's performance will improve?

- Why should I believe the information I have before me is accurate?

To become and *be*, you must execute!

Index

Get the eBook for only $10!

Now you can take the weightless companion with you anywhere, anytime. Your purchase of this book entitles you to 3 electronic versions for only $10.

This Apress title will prove so indispensible that you'll want to carry it with you everywhere, which is why we are offering the eBook in 3 formats for only $10 if you have already purchased the print book.

Convenient and fully searchable, the PDF version enables you to easily find and copy code—or perform examples by quickly toggling between instructions and   applications. The MOBI format is ideal for your Kindle, while the ePUB can be utilized on a variety of mobile devices.

Go to www.apress.com/promo/tendollars to purchase your companion eBook.

Other CA Press Titles You Will Find Useful

Developing B2B Social Communities
Brooks/Lovett/Creek
978-1-4302-4713-5

The Innovative CIO
Mann/Watt/Matthews
978-1-4302-4410-3

Service Virtualization
Michelsen/English
978-1-4302-4671-8

Cloud Standards
Waschke
978-1-4302-4110-2

APM Best Practices
Sydor
978-1-4302-3141-7

Agile Marketing
Accardi-Petersen
978-1-4302-3315-2

Eliminating "Us and Them"
Romero
978-1-4302-3644-3

Running Mainframe z on Distributed Platforms
Barrett/Norris
978-1-4302-6430-9

Under Control
Lamm
978-1-4302-1592-9

Available at www.apress.com

CPSIA information can be obtained at www.ICGtesting.com
Printed in the USA
BVOW04s2152151214

379572BV00001B/1/P